THE HERITAGE OF STEAM

2425
SOUT

THE HERITAGE OF STEAM

A family railway album

Illustrated with photographs by the author and his father, the late Arthur Davenport

Silver Link Publishing Ltd

625.261
DAV

© Arthur Neil Davenport 1995

All rights reserved. No part of this publication may be reproduced, stored in a retrieval system or transmitted, in any form or by any means, electronic, mechanical, photocopying, recording or otherwise, without prior permission in writing from Silver Link Publishing Ltd.

First published in 1995
Reprinted 2002

British Library Cataloguing in Publication Data

A catalogue record for this book is available from the British Library.

ISBN 1 85794 177 2

Frontispiece One of the second group of D. Earle Marsh's LB&SCR 'Atlantics', SR No 2425 *Trevose Head*, in lined malachite green livery, being coaled at New Cross Gate on 2 April 1949 (see also pages 174-6). This locomotive was built at Brighton in 1911 and classified 'H2'. Note the coal falling off the tender!

Silver Link Publishing Ltd
The Trundle
Ringstead Road
Great Addington
Kettering
Northants
NN14 4BW

Tel/Fax: 01536 330588
email: sales@nostalgiacollection.com
Website: www.nostalgiacollection.com

Printed and bound in Great Britain

The right of Arthur Neil Davenport to be identified as the author of this work has been asserted in accordance with sections 77 and 78 of the Copyright, Designs and Patents Act 1988.

Title page **My father was regular visitor to the East Coast Main line between 1952 and 1961. On Saturday 26 April 1952 he photographed Gresley Class 'K3' 2-6-0 No 61836 on a down freight train at Greenwood. The LNER 'K3' Class locomotives were introduced by the GNR early in 1920 and were the first to have what became the standard Gresley derived valve motion for actuating the piston valves of the inside (third) cylinder. Almost 200 were built for the LNER between 1924 and 1937, and they were used for express passenger, as well as goods, trains.** *AD*

Acknowledgements

While writing my text and captions I consulted the many books and articles included in the Bibliography on pages 189-90. I thank the authors for the help and pleasure their work has given me. I also thank my sister Jean for typing the manuscript.

Preface

In *Days of Steam* (Patrick Stephens Ltd, 1991) I presented photographs that my father and I had taken during the steam era on the railways of Great Britain. That book contained only a fraction of the pictures we had taken, and I was therefore delighted when Silver Link Publishing Ltd agreed to publish this further selection of our work. I hope that the pictures I have chosen will induce nostalgia in those who remember everyday steam on British railways and inspire younger enthusiasts of the preservation movement.

Contents

PLATFORM
3
13
32

Introduction

My father, Arthur Davenport (1893-1973), was born into a railway family. His father and both his grandfathers worked for the Midland Railway. Grandfather Henry Davenport (1829-1904) was manager of the Bromsgrove Station Works, which made and repaired wagons; he lived at 'Station Villa' nearby. He and his wife, Anne Maria, had eight children. Four survived into adulthood, and the youngest of these was Arthur Davenport (senior, 1862-1944), my grandfather. He started his working life as assistant timekeeper at the Bromsgrove works in 1878 and ultimately became Chief Timber Inspector of the London Midland & Scottish Railway (LMS), based at the Carriage & Wagon Department, Derby. He retired at the end of 1927.

Henry Davenport's daughter Rosa married Henry Sassons, and they had four daughters who settled in Bromsgrove. My father kept in touch with these cousins throughout his life and when he visited them was usually able to see and photograph trains on the famous Lickey Incline, which rises at the gradient of 1 in 37.7 from Bromsgrove to Blackwell, a distance of just over 2 miles.

My father's other grandfather was Thomas Woodward (1840-1925), who became Signal Engineer and Superintendent of the Midland Railway at Derby. During the latter part of his career he lived at Borrowash, 4 miles east-south-east of Derby, but in the 1870s, during construction of the Settle-Carlisle line, he lived at Appleby. My grandmother, Alice Maud Hannah (1870-1948), his second child by his second marriage, therefore spent several years of her childhood in that beautiful town. She revisited Appleby both before and after marrying my grandfather Davenport, in 1891, and they took my father there for holidays. He particularly remembered seeing

Left **Class '02' 0-4-4T No 32 *Bonchurch* on the train from Freshwater at Newport station during the Imperial College Railway Society (ICRS) tour of the Isle of Wight railways on Friday 24 March 1950. Twenty-three locomotives of this William Adams 1889 design for the L&SWR were used on the island. From 1932 onwards, larger bunkers holding 3 (instead of 1½) tons were fitted to all of them. They were numbered from 14 to 36 and named after places in the island.**

Below **In July 1947 our family summer holiday was spent at Llandudno in North Wales. My father photographed this LMS Compound on a train in the terminus; No 1119 was built at Horwich in 1925 and withdrawn in 1958.** *AD*

the first Midland Compound 4-4-0s, Nos 2631 and 2632, in their beautiful crimson lake livery.

My father was educated at St James's Church School and Derby School (founded in 1554). Surprisingly, he did not maintain the family tradition and follow a railway career. He was apprenticed to the National Provincial Bank and started work at the Lincoln Branch in January 1910. In September 1913 he was moved nearer home, to the branch at Burton-on-Trent, where he worked until joining the Royal Marine Artillery (a land-based unit of the Marines that no longer exists) in November 1915.

During the First World War he was stationed in Egypt from May 1916 to January 1917, helping to man naval guns deployed to discourage German submarines from entering that end of the Mediterranean. From April 1917 until Armistice Day, 11 November 1918, he served on 15-inch howitzer batteries in France and Belgium. He was demobilised in February 1919.

After leaving the Marines, father worked for six months at his old branch of the bank at Burton-on-Trent, and was then, in September 1919, transferred to the City Office in Bishopsgate where he worked for the rest of his career. From March 1934 until retirement in June 1953 he was Head of Bill Department.

During his first few years at the City Office, my father lived at Beckenham, but he settled in Epsom after marrying my mother, Doris Ferguson, daughter of a draughtsman who, like so many of my other forebears, worked at Derby for the Midland Railway. It was in Church Road, Epsom, that my sister Jean and I were born, and Epsom is the place where we still live.

For many of our holidays before the Second World War we were taken to see our grandparents. My father's parents remained in Derby but my mother's parents, John Young Ferguson and Maud Elizabeth (née King), moved from there to Ambergate and later to Bakewell, both places set in the beautiful Derbyshire countryside. For other country holidays we went to Appleby, which stands on the river Eden some 3 miles from the Pennine mountains. These were the holidays that founded our love of the north of England. For seaside we were taken to Scarborough and Ayr.

From early childhood I was encouraged by my father to share his interest in railways. The train journeys of our holidays became as enjoyable as the holidays themselves, and I got to know well the types of locomotives that worked, and the scenery of, the old Midland main lines from St Pancras to Derby and to Leeds and Appleby, including the most scenic part of the Settle-Carlisle line. Not surprisingly, the LMS became my favourite of the 'Big Four' companies, with the London & North Eastern Railway (LNER) running a close second.

Between holidays my interest in railways was sustained by occasional visits to London termini, by reading the *Railway Magazine*, by playing with my gauge O Hornby railway, and by drawing pictures of steam engines and trains. Unfortunately I did not take an interest in the Epsom railway scene, which until 1938 included steam services to the South Coast via the mid-Sussex line through Horsham and Arundel. I must have seen much Southern Railway (SR) steam activity in the years 1934 to 1942 walking to and from the Orchard School (a kindergarten) and the still flourishing Kingswood House preparatory school.

It was during my years at Epsom College (1942-1945) that my school friend Derek Lee and his father opened my eyes to the interest of the local railways. From 1943 onwards I went by rail or cycle on many train-watching expeditions, and my knowledge of the locomotives I saw was much increased when Ian Allan published his first 'ABCs' - illustrated booklets giving the names, numbers, designers and technical details of all the engines of the LMS, LNER, GWR and SR.

I left Epsom College at the end of the Summer Term 1945, not many months after the end of the Second World War in Europe, and went to study chemistry at the Royal College of Science in South Kensington. This is one of the colleges forming part of Imperial College, the full title of which, in those days, was the Imperial College of Science and Technology. On 1 August 1988 Imperial College merged with St Mary's Hospital Medical School, Paddington, and the full title became the Imperial College of Science, Technology and Medicine. The other constituents of Imperial College are the City and Guilds College, which teaches engineering, and the Royal School of Mines.

In 1946 a group of enthusiasts founded a railway society and I joined at once. The Imperial College Railway Society arranged lectures by distinguished speakers, including the late O. S. Nock, who was a graduate of the City and Guilds College and President of the Society from 1947 to 1950. It also arranged visits to places of interest, including locomotive works and sheds, and signal boxes. It was the opportunities for photography afforded by these visits that made me decide, in December 1947, to take up photography.

Photography was not a new hobby for the family. Both my parents took and processed their own pictures before their marriage, and during my childhood I was used to seeing my father developing and printing his films. He developed a film by inspection in red safelighting, seesawing it through MQ developer in a dish until the images appeared at the back of the opaque emulsion layer, showing that development had taken place throughout the thickness of the layer. He then rinsed the film in water, seesawed it through a hypo solution until the emulsion layer became transparent, washed the film in running water and dried it hanging straight from a line. The hypo dissolved the undeveloped light-sensitive silver halide from the emulsion and so fixed the images and allowed the film to be washed and dried in ordinary light. He cut the dry film into separate negatives.

My father contact-printed his negatives on printing-

Above One of the few railway photographs my father took before the Second World War - probably in August 1926. It shows a train on the Ashover Light Railway, a 2-foot-gauge line in Derbyshire that ran for 7¼ miles from Clay Cross to Ashover. The line was opened for goods traffic in the spring of 1924, and for passengers on 6 April 1925. Lieut-Col H. F. Stephens was consulting engineer. The locomotive *Guy* was built in November 1916 by the Baldwin Locomotive Company of Philadelphia, USA, and had been War Department No 525 during the First World War. The line survived until 1950. *AD*

Below The Robert Stephenson & Hawthorns 0-4-0ST, Works No 7349, obtained by the LCC in March 1947 to work the Horton Estate Light Railway and photographed by me on 11 April of that year. The line was used for taking coal from Ewell West, on the Wimbledon-Epsom line of the Southern Railway, to the Long Grove and West Park hospitals and the central power station. It was closed and dismantled in 1950.

out paper. A sheet of the paper was exposed through a negative to skylight until an image just darker than that desired in the final print was obtained. During exposure the negative and paper were pressed together between the glass and spring back of a contact printing frame. A hinged portion of the back could be lifted to allow the image to be inspected from time to time. After the exposure, he bathed the print in hypo solution to fix the image, washed it in water and allowed it to dry. Prints made in this way on 'Seltona' paper had attractive sepia images.

Until September 1939, when the onset of the Second World War made film no longer available, my father mainly took landscapes and pictures of the family. Although interested in railways from his boyhood, he had satisfied his hunger for railway pictures with commercial postcards and illustrations in the *Railway Magazine*. He therefore took very few railway photographs between the wars. These have always been of particular interest to me and I include two of them in this book.

Having decided to take railway photographs for myself, I looked out my mother's 'Vest Pocket Kodak' camera (VPK) which had an f 7.7 'Kodak' Anastigmat lens and a shutter giving only two speeds: 1/25 and 1/50 second. This used 127 size films providing eight negatives 2½ x 1⅝ inches in size. Unfortunately, the bellows had developed pinholes and almost all the negatives from my first two films were spoilt. Nevertheless the two most important negatives were only slightly fogged. They are of the last two engines used on the Horton Light Railway, a line used until 1949 to take coal wagons from the Southern Railway at Ewell West to mental hospitals at Epsom. The line was dismantled in 1950.

In September 1947 Kodak replaced the bellows in 'my' VPK and refocused the lens. Thereafter it gave excellent results as numbers of pictures in this book show. I fitted the camera with a direct-vision viewfinder - one intended for a Coronet 'Cub' camera - to make it easier to use.

In September 1948 I bought a second-hand Zeiss-Ikon 'Ikonta 520' camera with f 3.5 'Novar' lens in a 'Compur-Rapid' shutter (top speed 1/500 second). It gave 16 2¼ x 1⅝-inch negatives on a 120 or (purportedly) 620 film. The first pictures I took with it were disappointing, but after attention by a Wallace Heaton mechanic and - a little later - refocusing of the lens on the basis of photographic tests (by me), I obtained much better results.

My first few films were developed and printed commer-

On 9 September 1947 my father and I visited Carlisle Kingmoor and Upperby sheds during a holiday at Appleby, then county town of Westmorland. He photographed this former Caledonian Railway '3P' 4-6-0, of Pickersgill's '60' Class. It was No 63 before being renumbered by the LMS as 14653. A further 20 locomotives were added to the original batch of six during 1925-6. *AD*

cially. When I attempted to develop a film my father's way, I was not altogether successful, so I bought a developing tank. Use of a tank was essential for processing the panchromatic films (sensitive to all colours of light and so fogged by a red safelight), which gradually superseded the earlier blue- and green-sensitive 'orthochromatic' films. The latter reproduced a red buffer beam unrealistically as a dark tone, whereas panchromatic films, such as Kodak 'Super-XX' and Ilford HP3, reproduced red as a light tone and had the additional advantage of being faster. However, films - especially those of 127 size - were so scarce in those days that I gratefully bought whatever was available, regardless of make or type.

While at Imperial College I joined the Photographic Society and learned how to make enlargements. For my birthday in 1949 I was given money to buy an enlarging lens and other parts, which I used for making my own enlarger together with a safelight and processing dishes. The total cost was just over £14! I only enlarged selected pictures and made contact prints, on Kodak 'Velox' paper, of all my negatives for display in albums. It was not until 1953 that I started enlarging all negatives and abandoned contact printing.

Because of my interest in photography I applied during my last year at college (1950) for a job in the Research Laboratories of Kodak Ltd at The Works, Wealdstone. I was successful and worked there from 1 January 1951 onwards. In 1952 I completed a thesis on research that I had done during my last two years at college and obtained a PhD in physical chemistry.

For most of my time in the Harrow area I lived near Belmont Circle, close to Belmont, the intermediate station on the steam-worked branch from Harrow & Wealdstone to Stanmore Village. Thus I could easily get by train to Euston or to Watford Junction and beyond.

In June 1962 I accepted an opportunity to work for six months in the Kodak Patents and Trade Marks Department in High Holborn, and then - if the Department was willing to accept me - decide whether to stay there or return to the Research Laboratories. I decided to stay and in 1974 qualified as a patent agent. I continued to work in High Holborn until the end of April 1985, when I accepted an offer of early retirement made

The greatest recent loss to the Epsom railway scene was the demolition at the beginning of March 1993 of the signal box spanning the lines between the two island platforms of the 1929 station. The demolition was unexpected because the box was a listed building and the roof had been repaired in October 1989, only months before closure on 29 July 1990. This picture shows Class 'U' 2-6-0 No 31626 running tender-first towards Epsom Goods and London on 16 December 1962.

when the company decided to move the Patent Department from London to the Wealdstone site.

On starting work in High Holborn I resumed home life at Epsom, and while commuting saw the last 5½ years of steam services from Waterloo.

In June 1962 I bought a second-hand Zeiss Ikon 'Super-Ikonta 531' camera with a 7.5 cm f 3.5 'Tessar' lens, focused by rangefinder, in a 'Compur-Rapid' shutter. This lens, which a previous owner had had coated, gave significantly sharper negatives than those produced by the 'Novar' lens of the 'Ikonta 520'.

To complete the information about the cameras used for taking the pictures in this book, I must tell of those used by my father. After demobilisation in 1919 he first used a 'Vest Pocket Kodak' camera. For a short time he used a quarter-plate roll film camera giving eight 4¼ x 3¼-inch negatives per film, but he then settled on using the more practical 2¼ x 3¼-inch negative size of 120 film. His camera was a Butcher's 'Watch Pocket Carbine' with a 'Compur' shutter speeded from 1 second to 1/250th of a second and a 9 cm f 4.5 Ross 'Xpres' lens. In 1949 he part-exchanged that camera for a new Ensign 'Selfix 820' camera with a 13 cm f 3.8 Ross 'Xpres' lens in an 'Epsilon' shutter (top speed 1/250 second). Seven years later he bought an Ensign 'Selfix' 16-20 camera with a 7.5 cm f 3.5 Ross 'Xpres' lens in an 'Epsilon' shutter (top speed 1/300 second). This camera gave, as its code number indicates, 16 pictures on 120 size film and was smaller and lighter than the 'Selfix 8-20' camera. For the penalty of a very slight loss of image quality, my father halved his film consumption and produced negatives the whole area of which he could enlarge in my enlarger.

The camera used for taking any particular picture in this book can be found using the table below. The caption of each photograph taken by my father ends with his initials AD. The remainder were taken by me (AND in the table).

	Date of photograph	Camera used
AD	Up to 1949	Butcher's Carbine
AD	Apr 1950 to Jan 1956	Ensign 'Selfix 8-20'
AD	Feb 1956 onwards	Ensign 'Selfix 16-20'
AND	Apr 1947 to Sep 1948	'Vest Pocket Kodak'
AND	Oct 1948 to May 1962	Zeiss Ikon 'Ikonta 520'
AND	June 1962 onwards	Zeiss Ikon 'Super Ikonta 531'

The photographs that follow are arranged into five main groups. The first group contains pictures taken in and around interesting railway centres, of which Edinburgh, capital city of Scotland, is the most important. The second group shows trains in action on main lines of the former 'Big Four' companies. The third group illustrates a selection of branch lines. The fourth group contains pictures of a variety of locomotive types, three-quarters of them dating from before the 1923 Grouping, taken during visits to motive power depots. The fifth group shows some pre-Grouping semaphore signals.

1. Railway centres

Edinburgh

Edinburgh, the beautiful capital city of Scotland, stands near the southern shore of the Firth of Forth. The Old Town grew up along a ridge that runs from level ground near the Palace of Holyroodhouse upwards and westwards to the high rock that carries the castle. The thoroughfare between palace and castle is known as the 'Royal Mile'.

Just north of the Old Town is a valley in which there used to be a lake - the Nor' Loch. This was drained in 1760, and in 1772 the North Bridge was built across the valley to encourage development of the land to the north. This duly took place during the remaining years of the century and resulted in the handsome New Town. Princes Street, parallel to the Royal Mile, and named after the sons of George III, forms the southern boundary and, through having buildings only on its northern side, affords a splendid view of the castle.

When, in the mid-1840s, railway companies reached the centre of Edinburgh from east and west, their station was in the valley between the Old and New Towns, near to the North Bridge. By 1854 this station had been named 'Waverley' after the series of novels by Sir Walter Scott. During construction of the New Town, the valley along which the railway now runs had been partly filled with builders' spoil, to form 'The Mound', so trains from the west pass through tunnels shortly before entering the Waverley station.

When the Forth Bridge was opened in 1890, Edinburgh Waverley became too small to handle all the traffic, so the North British Railway (NBR) rebuilt the station between 1892 and 1897, and it became, for a time, the largest station in the United Kingdom. Most of the area occupied by its 21 platforms was covered by a glass roof. The story goes that when a countryman who had visited Edinburgh for the first time, by train, was asked what he thought of the city, he had replied: 'It's a fine place; it's all covered in!'

During the 19th century three rail routes developed between London and Edinburgh. The earliest (1848) was the London & North Western Railway (LNWR) West Coast Route from Euston to Carlisle then from Carlisle to Edinburgh on the Caledonian Railway (CR). The next (1852) was the East Coast Route from King's Cross to York on the Great Northern (GNR), from York to Berwick on the North Eastern (NER) and from Berwick to Edinburgh on the North British. This route did not attain its present form until 1870 when the NER opened a more direct line through Selby to its junction with the GNR at Shaftholme. The third route (1876) was from St Pancras to Carlisle on the Midland Railway (MR), via Leeds and the newly opened Settle-Carlisle line, then from Carlisle to Edinburgh over the NBR's 'Waverley Route' through Hawick. The North British stages of the East Coast trains and Midland services from London ended their journeys in the Waverley station, but West Coast trains were taken by the Caledonian Railway from Carlisle into an Edinburgh terminus of its own. There were, successively, three of these, just south of the west end of Princes Street. The third and last, named Princes Street, existed from 1894 to 1965.

I spent two separate weeks of holiday in Edinburgh during the steam era. The first was with my parents in August 1948; the second was with all the family in July 1950. The journeys were so interesting that I give details below.

In 1948 we travelled both ways by the 'Queen of Scots'. This Pullman express had regained its pre-war title only a month earlier, in July. The train formation going north was, starting at the King's Cross buffer-stops and using the letters employed for seat reservation, as follows: 'A', 'B' and 'C' - 3rd Class Cars Nos 78, 71 and 76; 'D' - 'Sheila'; 'E' - 'Evadne'; 'F', 'G' and 'H' - 3rd Class Cars Nos 84, 58 and 80; 'J' - 'Agatha'; and 'K' - 3rd Class Car No 67. I remember the dull green fluted upholstery of the seats, and also the splendid meals served from time to time. However, what made our luxurious journey even more memorable was the fact that it took place only a day after torrential rain on 11 and 12 August had blocked the East Coast Main Line at 11 places between Newcastle and Edinburgh and also the Waverley route at Galashiels and elsewhere. The 'Queen of Scots' was therefore rerouted from Newcastle through Carlisle to Carstairs, then on to Princes Street. The motive power was as follows:

King's Cross to Leeds (Central): 'A3' 'Pacific' No 60059 *Tracery*
Leeds to Newcastle: 'V2' 2-6-2 No 918
Newcastle to Carstairs: 'A3 'Pacific' No 77 *The White Knight*
Carstairs to Princes Street: '4P' 2-6-4T No 2269

Leeds (Central) station, closed at the end of April 1967, was a terminus, and cars 'J' and 'K' were left behind there when the train departed for Newcastle.

The return journey was equally interesting. The train went south to St Boswells and along single track to Kelso, then on to Tweedmouth to join the normal East Coast route. We saw many people on the branch-line stations and bridges watching the handsome train go by.

The train formation going south was: 'A', 'B' and 'C' - 3rd Class Cars Nos 77, 106 and 75; 'D' - 'Juana'; 'E' - 'Joan'; 'F', 'G', 'H' and 'J' - 3rd Class Cars Nos 83, 81, 79 and 67; and 'K' - 'Agatha'. Cars 'J' and 'K' were added to the train at Leeds (Central).

The motive power was:

Edinburgh Waverley to Newcastle: 'A3' 'Pacific' No 60029 *Woodstock*
Newcastle to Leeds (Central): 'B1' 4-6-0 No 1224
Leeds (Central) to King's Cross: 'A3' 'Pacific' No 60059 *Tracery*

It is noteworthy that only the two 'A3' 'Pacifics' had been given British Railways numbers by the addition of 60000.

Our 1950 holiday was for two weeks, the first spent at Hawes in Wensleydale and the second in Edinburgh. We travelled on former Midland Railway lines and the Waverley route. Going north on 1 July we broke our journey at Hellifield to visit the locomotive shed.

The motive power was:

9.50 am St Pancras to Leeds: 'Jubilee' 4-6-0 No 45640 *Frobisher*
Leeds to Hellifield: not noted
Hellifield to Garsdale: Class '5' 4-6-0 No 44900
Garsdale to Hawes: Class 'G5' 0-4-4T No 67346

Continuing to Edinburgh on 8 July we travelled behind:

8.56 am Hawes to Garsdale: Class 'G5' 0-4-4T No 67324
9.16 am Garsdale to Carlisle: 'Jubilee' 4-6-0 No 45597 *Barbados*
1.25 pm Carlisle to Edinburgh: 'A3' 'Pacific' No 60079 *Bayardo*

I failed to record all the numbers of the locomotives used for the return journey, but did note that Class '5' 4-6-0 No 44891 on the Leeds-St Pancras stretch was given a '4F' 0-6-0 goods engine as a pilot from Wellingborough onwards, and that the train reached St Pancras at 10.05 pm, 48 minutes late!

During both our Edinburgh holidays we stayed at an hotel near Newington station on the Southside Suburban circle, and travelled on that line a number of times. The train services had been introduced by the North British Railway in 1884 and were withdrawn by British Railways in 1962 after four final years' operation with diesel multiple units.

In 1948 we obtained permission to visit St Margaret's shed, the former LNER depot that supplied locomotives for the many branch-line and goods workings in the district. In 1950 we had permits not only for St Margaret's but also for the other two principal sheds, Haymarket (ex-LNER) and Dalry Road (ex-LMS). Some of the pictures we took on these visits are presented in the fourth main section of this book.

On both holidays we visited the Forth Bridge and in 1950 went to North Berwick to see the town and enjoy the well-nigh obligatory sail around the Bass Rock. The Forth Bridge deserves its reputation as being one of the engineering marvels of the world. Photographs, such as those I present in this book, give a fine idea of its structure but little idea of its size. To appreciate that, one has to stand nearby and tip one's head right back to view the underside of the approach viaducts, or to go on to the Forth Road Bridge upstream.

Class 'A3' 'Pacific' No 60059 *Tracery* backing on to the 'Queen of Scots' Pullman at Leeds (Central) during our homeward journey on Friday 20 August 1948. This station was closed in 1967 when all traffic was transferred to a rebuilt Leeds City station.

The beautiful view over Edinburgh that one has from the castle. A Thompson 'A2' 'Pacific' is pulling a train of compartment stock out of the Mound Tunnel, and is just about to pass under the first of the footbridges that used to link the north and south portions of the Princes Street gardens. The buildings on The Mound are the Royal Scottish Academy and, to its right, the National Gallery of Scotland. Behind the latter is the Gothic Scott Monument, 200 feet high, on the south side of Princes Street. In the distance are the port of Leith, the Firth of Forth and, to the right, the Calton Hill with its unfinished copy of the Parthenon and Nelson's monument. The picture was taken on Sunday 9 July 1950.

Left A former North British Railway (NBR) 4-4-0 designed by Reid and built 1909-10 as No 894. It was renumbered by the LNER after 1924 as 9894 ('D33') and became 2459 in the 1946 renumbering scheme. The additional initial '6' shown in the picture was added by British Railways. The train is standing at the west end of Waverley station on Monday 10 July 1950. The North British Station Hotel is in the background; opened in 1902, since 1991 it has been named the Balmoral Forte Grand.

Above LNER, former NBR, Class 'D30/2' 4-4-0 No 2429 *The Abbot* at Waverley station on Monday 16 August 1948. The 27 locomotives of the second series of the 'Scott' Class were designed by Reid and built from 1912 to 1920. The shed name painted on the buffer beam below the engine number is Thornton.

Below Two former NBR Reid 4-4-0s at the Waverley station at 9.40 am on Friday 20 August 1948. The nearer is No 2405 *The Fair Maid* of the original 'Scott' Class, LNER Class 'D29', built 1909-11; the farther is No 62488 *Glen Aladale* of the ex-NBR 'Glen' Class built 1913-20. LNER Class 'D34' *Glen Douglas*, which became BR No 62469, has been preserved as NBR No 256 in its original livery. In the background is the National Gallery of Scotland, built on The Mound.

Above Ex-NBR Reid 0-6-0 goods engine No 64501 at Edinburgh Waverley on Monday August 16 1948. This engine of LNER Class 'J35' was built in the period 1906-13, and before the 1946 renumbering was No 9371. The last of the 'J35s' was withdrawn in 1962.

Below Unnamed Thompson 'B1' 4-6-0 No 61117 in LNER green livery hauls the up 'Queen of Scots' Pullman from Glasgow out of the Mound Tunnel on Monday 10 July 1950. On the skyline above the locomotive boiler is Edinburgh Castle. The character near the end of the platform is the author, who had just taken a picture. *AD*

Above Class 'A2/1' 'Pacific' No 60509 *Waverley* arrives at the Waverley station on Monday 10 July 1950. The placing of the outside cylinders behind the bogie and the use of a rimless chimney spoiled, for this author, the appearance of this Thompson design of 1944. The electrically illuminated ground signals, seen from the rear, date from the mid-1930s electric resignalling.

Below Gresley Class 'A3' 'Pacific' No 60066 *Merry Hampton* emerges from the Mound Tunnel with a train of varnished teak stock on the same day. The raised patch at the top rear of the smokebox, covering the superheater header, and the elongated dome are the main visible differences between the 'A3' and the original 'A1' (later 'A10') 'Pacifics'.

A westbound train emerges from the other end of the Mound Tunnel on Friday 14 July 1950. The locomotive is No 62693 *Roderick Dhu* of LNER Class 'D11/2', introduced in 1924. The design was based on Robinson's 1920 'Large Director' Class of the Great Central Railway and built to the Scottish loading gauge. The end of a Waverley station platform is visible through the right-hand tunnel. The picture was taken from the footbridge, loved by train watchers and photographers, shown in my view from Edinburgh Castle. *AD*

Above The station pilot at Edinburgh Waverley on Tuesday 17 August 1948 was Class 'J83' 0-6-0T No 8474; designed by Holmes for the NBR, it was built as No 826 in 1900-1. It stands in the beautiful apple green livery with black and white lining and gold lettering that was intended for all LNER locomotives just before nationalisation.

Below At the eastern end of Waverley station on Saturday 15 July 1950 is Class 'A1' 'Pacific' No 60159, later named *Bonnie Dundee*. This Peppercorn class was based on Thompson's 1945 rebuild of Gresley's first 'Pacific', GNR No 1470 *Great Northern* of 1922. It looks as if the man in the right foreground is about to replace a point motor.

Above Ex-War Department 2-8-0 No 90289, of Riddles design, and a brake-van pass eastbound through Newington station on the Edinburgh Southside Suburban line on Monday 10 July 1950.

Below On the same day Gresley Class 'V1' 2-6-2T No 67617 enters Newington station on an eastbound train round the Southside Suburban line. The shed name on the buffer beam is St Margaret's.

Above Another Class 'V1' 2-6-2T enters Gorgie station on the Southside Suburban line on Friday 14 July 1950. The engine carries its BR No 67659 and shed plate 64A (St Margaret's). We travelled to Newington in this train.

Below A third 'V1' 2-6-2T from St Margaret's shed standing in North Berwick station on the train by which we returned to Edinburgh Waverley on Wednesday 12 July 1950. The North Berwick branch joins the East Coast Main Line at Drem, about 16 miles east of Waverley.

A train of four-wheeled carriages in Edinburgh Princes Street station on Friday 14 July 1950. These were the nearest thing that I ever saw to my Hornby gauge O railway carriages and had the numbers 26057, 26066, 26069, 26073, 26085 and 26092, the two last being composite coaches. They were used for services on the Leith branch.

Gresley class 'V1' 2-6-2T No 67630 in Leith Central station on Tuesday 11 July 1950. This was Edinburgh's third largest station and was built by the North British Railway as a condition for the refusal by the authorities to give the Caledonian Railway permission to build a line to Leith under Princes Street and the Calton Hill. The station was opened on 1 July 1903 and closed in April 1952. It was later used as a diesel maintenance depot, and demolished in 1989.

Ex-NBR 0-4-0ST No 68092, designed by Holmes, LNER Class 'Y9', with its wooden tender 'Loco Dept South Leith 971555'. It was shunting in the docks at Leith on Tuesday 11 July 1950.

A southbound train hauled by 'Scott' Class 4-4-0 No 62412 *Dirk Hatteraick* (LNER Class 'D29') about to leave North Queensferry station and cross the Forth Bridge. Note the Forth Bridge North signal box and the pre-Grouping lower quadrant signals. The Forth Bridge was built between April 1883 and 1890, the opening ceremony being on 4 March of the latter year. It was designed by Sir John Fowler and Mr (later Sir) Benjamin Baker, and Allan D. Steward, a Cambridge mathematician, was almost certainly responsible for the basic calculations. The bridge contains over 50,000 tons of steel and its overall length is 2,768 yards - more than a mile and a half. *AD*

Another southbound train at North Queensferry on the approach viaduct to the Forth Bridge. This has ten spans, is 1,980 feet long, and the track is carried 157 feet above high water. The locomotive appears to be a 'Scott' Class 4-4-0 and the fourth carriage of the train is in the then new bright red and cream livery.

The *Granton* passenger and vehicle ferry at North Queensferry on Friday 14 July 1950. The mile-long trip across the Firth of Forth gave splendid views of the bridge. The name 'Granton' is that of the port just north of Edinburgh from which in the days before the Forth Bridge, between 1847 and 1890, railway passengers and freight for the north were taken by ferry to Burntisland.

Bromsgrove

Bromsgrove, in Worcestershire, is on the former LMS line from Birmingham to Bristol. Three companies were involved in its building; the first was the Birmingham & Gloucester Railway, which opened a standard (4 ft 8½ in) gauge line from Bromsgrove to Cheltenham on 24 June 1840. By 17 December of that year the necessary links between Birmingham and Bromsgrove and between Cheltenham and Gloucester had been completed.

The second company involved was the Bristol & Gloucester Railway, which had been persuaded by the Great Western Railway to build its line to Brunel's broad (7 ft 0¼ in) gauge. It opened for passengers on 8 July 1844, and its trains used the lines of the third company, the broad gauge Cheltenham & Great Western Union Railway, for about 7 miles between Standish Junction and Gloucester.

It was at Gloucester that the full inconvenience of a change of gauge in the middle of an important route was first experienced. On 9 July 1845 a Royal Commission was appointed to investigate the matter and it concluded (doubtless having been impressed by a well-staged scene of chaos) that future lines should be built to the standard gauge. This requirement was embodied in the Gauge Act of 1846, but this Act did not prevent the laying of any further broad gauge track because it allowed future enactments to provide for the use of non-standard gauges in particular instances.

On 14 January 1845 the Birmingham & Gloucester and Bristol & Gloucester companies agreed to amalgamate. Before Parliamentary approval for this merger had been obtained, the Great Western Railway entered into negotiations to acquire the two companies.

The Midland Railway heard of these negotiations through the Chairman, John Ellis, happening to travel in the same train as two Directors of the Gloucester companies. The MR was therefore able, as soon as the negotiations had failed, to arrange to buy both companies; they were absorbed into the Midland system by an Act of 1846. However, it was not until 1854 that the Midland was able to run standard gauge trains between Bristol and Gloucester.

One more sequence of events had an important influence on Bromsgrove's position as a railway centre. By an Act of 1845, Parliament sanctioned the building of the

One of the many 0-6-0 classes to work on the Lickey. Two '9400' Class 0-6-0 Pannier tanks wait for the 'off' signal at the new gantry near the south end of Bromsgrove station on Friday 27 October 1961; the nearer locomotive is No 9429. Bromsgrove South box and its junction signals are just visible in the distance. *AD*

Oxford, Worcester & Wolverhampton Railway. Originally, as a result of Great Western influence, this line was to have been mixed gauge, but it was in fact constructed to the standard gauge. The company built, in two stages, a loop to the west of the Birmingham & Gloucester main line. The first stage, from Abbots Wood Junction - some 12 miles south of Bromsgrove - to Worcester was opened on 5 October 1850. The second stage, from Worcester through Droitwich to Stoke Works Junction - about 2 miles south of Bromsgrove - was opened on 15 February 1852 (Stoke Works was an important salt works producing a lucrative goods traffic). From the outset passenger services on the loop through Worcester were operated by the Midland Railway (an arrangement continued through LMS into BR days) even though most of the line was part of the Great Western route from Oxford to Wolverhampton.

The Birmingham & Gloucester Railway had established its locomotive headquarters at Bromsgrove in 1840, and the Midland Railway developed the Station Works into a wagon repair shop. It became the second most important shop of the Railway, the first being the Derby Works. Bromsgrove Wagon Works was closed in 1964 and the work was transferred to the Derby Carriage & Wagon Works, Litchurch Lane.

Bromsgrove's fame as a railway centre derives not from the excellence of its Works, but from the fact that the station is at the foot of a 1 in 37.7 incline just over 2 miles long, the Lickey Incline. In steam days all but the lightest trains had to be banked up this incline. The heavier the train, the greater the number of banking engines used. The first bankers were five American 4-2-0s, built by William Norris of Philadelphia, of Class A (Extra) supplied in 1840 and 1842. But for having cylinders of 12 inches (instead of 11½ inches) diameter, they were similar to the Class A engines used over the whole of the line. In 1845 an 0-6-0T was designed by McConnell and built at the Birmingham & Gloucester Railway works at Bromsgrove, the first of many types of six-coupled engines to be used for banking.

The Lickey Banker was the 0-10-0 designed by Sir Henry Fowler specially for the job and completed at Derby in January 1920. This was equivalent in tractive effort (43,315 lbs) to two of the various types of 0-6-0T also used for banking. The very large 2-8-8-2 Beyer-Garratt, LNER Class 'U1' No 2395 (later BR No 69999), was used for a time. With a tractive effort of 72,940 lbs, this should have been sufficient for banking almost any train. However, it did not become popular with locomotive crews, both because of the large amount of coal that had to be shovelled during an ascent and because its power could have reduced the number of bankers, and so crews, needed.

The first of four 1,750 hp diesel-electric locomotives to be used for banking arrived on 2 July 1964, but some steam locomotives continued this work until June 1966.

My father took railway photographs at and around Bromsgrove on at least nine occasions, and I owe to him all the pictures that I have chosen to illustrate this section of the book.

Below 'Big Bertha', the Midland 'Lickey Banker', standing at the south end of Bromsgrove station on Thursday 8 December 1951. The locomotive's number when it first appeared in 1920 was 2290 and this was changed to 22290 in September 1947 and to 58100 in January 1949. It was withdrawn from service in May 1956 and cut up at Derby in June 1957. *AD*

Above right The only Beyer-Garratt locomotive built for the LNER by Beyer, Peacock & Co Ltd in 1925 to the design of Sir Nigel Gresley. This Class 'U1' locomotive, No 2395, became No 6999 under the 1946 renumbering scheme and became 69999 under BR in 1948. The locomotive was equivalent to two Gresley Class 'O2' three-cylinder 2-8-0s (the tractive effort being twice 36,470 lbs, or 72,940 lbs) and had wheels, cylinders and motion interchangeable with locomotives of that class. It did not prove popular with the Bromsgrove crews, however, and although it was converted to oil burning in 1952, it was taken out of its service at Bromsgrove in 1955 and scrapped in 1956. This photograph was taken at Bromsgrove shed in 1949. *AD*

Right English Electric Type 3 Co-Co 1,750 bhp diesel-electric locomotive No D6938 helping a '9400' Class Pannier tank bank a goods train up the Lickey Incline on Wednesday 19 August 1964. This was the first diesel locomotive to be provided for banking, arriving at Bromsgrove on 2 July 1964. The use of steam locomotives for banking ceased in June 1966. The diesel-electric shown was categorised as Class 37 in 1968 and subsequently renumbered 37 238. *AD*

69999

F15
D6938

The down 'Devonian' express from Bradford to Bristol, hauled by 'Black Five' No 44850, is seen passing the Midland 'Lickey Banker' No 58100 and Fowler 'Jinty' 0-6-0T No 4738 in this panorama of Bromsgrove South on 21 July 1950. The train earned its title of 1927 by including through carriages for Torquay and Paignton, worked by the GWR. Note the telegraph poles, a feature of the railway scene that has now vanished. *AD*

The 9.27 am train to Birmingham arrives at Bromsgrove station on 26 August 1958. The engine is Fowler Compound No 41123, built by the LMS in 1925 and withdrawn by BR in 1959. With Fowler 0-6-0T No 47276 providing assistance, the train then starts its journey up the Lickey Incline. Note the houses built since the 1950 photograph shown on page 33 was taken, and the replacement of the stone slabs of the platform with tarmac. *AD*

A train of 25 Esso oil tanks, spaced at each end from the motive power by a brake-van and two open wagons, moves from the up slow line into Bromsgrove station on 26 October 1961. The signal gantry replaced that shown on page 28. The train engine, No 92231, is a BR standard 2-10-0. The banking engines, shown below, are another 2-10-0, No 92234, an unidentified '9400' Class 0-6-0PT and 'Jinty' 0-6-0T No 47276, while the brake van is of Southern Railway design. *AD*

Another goods train, this time banked by a solitary Fowler '3F' 0-6-0T, sets off up the Lickey Incline on 21 July 1950. The upward bend of the train just beyond the road bridge is apparent, as is the good variety of parcels on the platform trolley waiting to travel in the guard's van of a passenger train. *AD*

One of the R. M. Deeley Midland Railway Compound 4-4-0s built in 1906 and withdrawn by BR in 1951, waits in Bromsgrove station to take a train up the Lickey Incline. It is in the early BR lined black livery and the first carriage is in the red and cream livery current at the date of the picture, 21 July 1950. The early Compounds had 7-foot driving wheels, while those built by Fowler for the LMS between 1924 and 1932 had 6 ft 9 in wheels. *AD*

Above A group of four banking engines seen from Newton bridge, to the south of Bromsgrove. The ex-GWR design Pannier tank is No 8402, one of the non-superheated members of the '9400' Class built after nationalisation from 1949 onwards. It was the first engine of the Class to be allocated to Bromsgrove shed (code 21C), arriving in August 1956. It is seen with 'Jinty' No 47303 and two others of that Class on 1 November 1956. *AD*

Below The 'Devonian' climbing up the Lickey Incline on Thursday 4 November 1954, assisted by two Fowler '3F' 0-6-0Ts. The train is passing Finstall churchyard, and the carriages are in the attractive red and cream livery of the period. *AD*

Stratford-on-Avon

Strictly speaking, the first railway at Stratford-on-Avon was the Stratford & Moreton Railway, opened in 1826, which ran 17 miles south to Moreton-in-Marsh. It was the only part completed of an ambitious scheme to link the canal system of the Midlands with London. The line was laid to 4-foot gauge with malleable iron rails on stone blocks and worked by horse traction. Its most attractive and useful relic is the brick bridge, now a footbridge, over the River Avon at Stratford.

The first conventional railway to Stratford was the Great Western. Brunel had opened his broad gauge main line from London, via Reading, Didcot and Swindon, to Bristol on 30 June 1841, and completed a branch from Didcot to Oxford in June 1844. That was extended via Leamington Spa to Birmingham in 1846 using mixed gauge track, an intermediate rail allowing passage of standard gauge trains. A branch from Hatton Junction, just beyond Leamington, reached Stratford on 10 October 1860.

Stratford was reached from the south on 11 July 1859 by a standard gauge branch from Honeybourne Junction on the Oxford, Worcester & Wolverhampton Railway. This standard gauge line had opened between Evesham and Wolvercot, near Oxford, on 4 June 1853, and was absorbed by the Great Western on 1 August 1863.

The provision of mixed gauge tracks from Oxford through Reading to Basingstoke on 22 December 1856, and from Reading into Paddington on 1 October 1861, showed that the broad gauge could not ultimately survive. However, it was to last about 30 years more, until 22 May 1892.

From 1 January 1873 Stratford-on-Avon was served by a second railway, the East & West Junction Railway, primarily intended for the conveyance of iron ore from Northamptonshire to South Wales. This traffic did not materialise until the start of the First World War in 1914 because until then ore was imported by sea from Spain. The traffic continued until the end of the war in 1918. It also existed throughout the Second World War (1939-45) and until the mid-1960s.

The East & West Junction Railway subsequently became part of the Stratford-upon-Avon & Midland Junction Railway (SMJR), formed on 1 January 1909, which in turn became part of the LMS on 1 January 1923 at the Grouping. The normal passenger service on the line was between Blisworth and Stratford. Trains, some continuing journeys to and from Blisworth, also ran between Stratford and Broom Junction on the Redditch to Evesham line. The final services, between Blisworth and Stratford, were withdrawn on Saturday 5 April 1952.

My sister and I stayed at Stratford-on-Avon in 1949, 1950 and 1951 to go to Shakespeare productions at the Memorial Theatre and to visit the local sites and countryside. We travelled each way by train, changing at Leamington Spa. In 1949 the train engines for the down journey, on Friday 9 September, were No 6008 *King James II* (on the 2.10 pm from Paddington) and No 4092 *Dunraven Castle* (on the 4.20 pm from Leamington). For the return journey, on Sunday 11 September, they were '5100' Class 2-6-2T No 4139 to Leamington and No 7005 *Sir Edward Elgar* from there to Paddington.

In 1950 we travelled on Friday 26 May by the 11.10 am train from Paddington behind No 6006 *King George I* and from Leamington to Stratford in railcar No 29 (with trailer coach). The return journey on Whit Monday, 29 May, was by the 5.45 pm from Stratford behind '2251' Class 0-6-0 goods No 2247, and from Leamington to Paddington behind No 5070 *Sir Daniel Gooch*.

Left A primitive illuminated 'Beware of Trains' sign above a cast-iron Stratford-upon-Avon & Midland Junction Railway sign on the east wall of the newer signal box at Stratford-upon-Avon ex-SMJR (LMS) station.

Above right Class '4F' 0-6-0 goods No 44185 in Stratford-on-Avon ex-SMJR station on 27 May 1950 in early British Railways livery. Compare the original signals with those shown in the picture below. The typical LMS station sign had a yellow circle-bar, with black lettering and edging, on a white background.

Right The new and old signal boxes at Stratford-on-Avon station on 7 October 1951. Notice the tubular-post home signal and dwarf shunting signals installed to replace the bracket signal shown in the picture above.

44185

STRATFORD-ON-AVON

44185

Left The abandoned old signal box and attractive station building on the up platform of Stratford-on-Avon, photographed on 27 May 1950. The fine canopy (which presumably spoiled the view from the original signal box) dates from after 1897, but the building proper would have been constructed for the opening of the East & West Junction Railway in 1873.

Below left The 11.58 am train to Blisworth, generously formed of two carriages, waits in Stratford-on-Avon station on Saturday 27 May 1950. The locomotive, No 44185, is that shown on page 37, while the light engine in the down platform is a '4F' of the MR 1911 design, No 43846.

Above Johnson/Deeley '3F' 0-6-0 No 43523 of 1885 design stands by the water-softening plant at Stratford ex-LMS engine shed on 27 May 1950; the engine taking water is No 44185. The shed was on the south side of the line, adjacent to the station, and could accommodate 14 locomotives. A turntable large enough to accommodate a Great Central 'Atlantic' was installed in 1908 to allow these engines to work excursions from Marylebone to Stratford via Woodford.

Right A close-up view of one of the ex-MR, LMS Class '4F', 0-6-0s in the locomotive yard at Stratford shed. Note the flared upper edge of the tender with coal rails and the LMS lettering. The code for Stratford-on-Avon shed, 21D, is seen on the small elliptical cast-iron plate fixed to the smokebox door. Part of the goods shed shows to the right of the engine.

Above We now move to the former GWR station at Stratford-on-Avon, where Class '5100' 2-6-2T No 4139 waits with an evening train for Leamington Spa. My sister and I travelled by this train during our journey back to Epsom on Sunday 11 September 1949; the dirt on the locomotive and carriage was typical of the era. Notice, between the column of the water-crane and the funnel for catching drips from the leather delivery pipe, a stove used for preventing freezing in winter. The distant gasholder would, in those days, have held coal-gas.

Below Another Class '5100' 2-6-2T, No 5180, at the south end of the ex-GWR station at Stratford. In the early days of British Railways the name was - as shown - painted in full on tank- or tender-side. The numbers of the former GWR locomotives were not changed, allowing the handsome brass numberplates to be retained. The LMS-style smokebox door numberplates were new, the numbers having originally been painted on the front buffer beam.

Above right A northbound train from Honeybourne behind Collett '2251' Class 0-6-0 No 2247 stands in Stratford-on-Avon station on Whit Monday, 29 May 1950. This engine was taken off the train, which continued its journey behind the locomotive in the background, '5100' Class 2-6-2T No 4157.

Right A northbound freight train runs through the station hauled by 2-6-0 No 9302 (subsequently renumbered 7324), one of the later members of the '4300' Class that were provided with side window cabs; No 9303 has been preserved. The train is about to obscure the large and informative station sign. Notice the track - bull-headed rails held in cast-iron chairs by wooden keys - the norm until after the Second World War. The short two-bolt fishplates joining the rails allowed the adjacent sleepers to be closer together than with the four-bolt variety.

STRATFORD ON AVON
GENERAL

Seen from a bridge over the line in the southern outskirts of Stratford-on-Avon, 'Bulldog' Class 4-4-0 No 3455 *Starling* takes a stopping train to Honeybourne on Saturday 27 May 1950. In the background is the level crossing with the A439 road to Evesham.

Above A former GWR 0-6-2T of the Collett '5600' Class, No 6632, on a southbound goods train just about to cross the River Avon about a mile to the south-west of Stratford. Nine locomotives of this class have been preserved.

Left A pre-Beeching casualty: Great Alne station on the Alcester to Bearley line north-west of Stratford, closed on 25 September 1939, shortly after the beginning of the Second World War, but used for workmen's trains until 3 July 1944. The washing makes me think of Buggleskelly station in the classic Will Hay film *Oh, Mr Porter!*.

Longmoor Military Railway

The Longmoor Military Railway (LMR) came into existence at an infantry camp built during the South African War of 1899 to 1902 at Longmoor, between Bordon and Liss in Hampshire. The 53rd Railway Company of the Royal Engineers undertook to move 68 huts from Longmoor to Bordon, 5 miles away, and did so by laying two 18-inch-gauge tramway tracks 24 feet (a hut's width) apart, putting each hut, in turn, on trolleys on the lines, and hauling it with mobile steam winches to its destination.

Between 1905 and 1909 a standard gauge railway was laid from Longmoor to Bordon, terminus of an L&SWR branch from Bentley opened on 1 June 1905. In 1906 the line was renamed the Woolmer Instructional Military Railway, but the original name was restored in 1935.

During the First World War a line from Longmoor to a bridge-building site at Hollywater was made. Between the wars, in the years 1930 to 1933, a 3½-mile extension to Liss on the SR Portsmouth main line was laid. A connection with that line and exchange sidings were provided in 1942, during the Second World War. In that year, also, the Hollywater line was extended to form the Hollywater Loop, a 6-mile circuit allowing continuous running. At its fullest state of development

Left Robert Stephenson & Hawthorns-built, Hunslet-designed 0-6-0ST No 75079 *Lisieux* (originally named *Sir John French* and later renumbered 114) suspended from the LMR 45-ton Ransome & Rapier steam breakdown crane at Longmoor Downs on Saturday 2 September 1950. Her works plate reads 'Robert Stephenson & Hawthorns Ltd. 7116 1943'. The weight of the locomotive would have been a few tons over the nominal 45-ton limit.

Right A passenger train from Liss approaches Longmoor Downs hauled by 0-6-0ST *Lisieux*, by then renumbered 114, on 5 September 1953. The train is on the 110-foot span No 6 bridge, which was substituted, in 1952, for a 100-foot bridge dating from the 1920s. The locomotive and train are painted blue with yellow lettering, the locomotive having red lining as well, together with vermilion buffer beams and backgrounds to the name and works plates. Concrete sleepers are heaped in the foreground. *AD*

the LMR had 12 miles of running line and about 60 miles of sidings.

Throughout its history the LMR was used for training Royal Engineers to lay, operate and maintain railway systems. Workshops capable of all but the heaviest engineering work were established. The line was also used as a depot at which railway materials could be stored. Some million tons of stores, including locomotives and rolling-stock, and thousands of personnel were handled before and after the Allied landings in France during 1944.

Presumably because of the vulnerability of railway systems to modern weapons, military interest in rail transportation declined in post-war years and the LMR was closed on 31 October 1969. The last Open Day had been held on 5 July that year. From early in 1968 onwards, an attempt to retain part of the LMR as a steam preservation centre was made, but objections from local residents prevented this from happening.

I visited the LMR on four occasions, taking photographs during the last three. The first occasion was on 16 April 1946 when the father of my friend Derek Lee took him and me, by car, to see the line. My notes show that we saw five War Department (WD) 2-10-0s, nine 2-8-0s, 67 Ministry of Supply 0-6-0STs of Hunslet design (but built by six different makers), two ex-LB&SCR Class 'I2' 4-4-2Ts, Nos 72400 *Earl Roberts* and 72401, four ex-GWR Dean 0-6-0 goods engines (No 70195 having pannier tanks as well as its tender), and named locomotives including 0-6-0Ts Nos 70203 *Sir John French*, 70204 *Selborne* and 70207 *Marlborough*, 0-6-2Ts Nos 70205 *Gordon* (from the Taff Vale Railway) and 70208 *Kitchener*, 0-6-0ST No 228 *Daisy*, 4-4-0T *Kingsley* from the M&GNJR, and 2-8-0 No 79250 *Major General McMullen*. Nearly all these numbers include the 70000 added in the latter part of 1944 to avoid confusion between the numbers of WD locomotives and those of other railways. LMR practices that increased, rather than diminished, confusion were the renumbering of WD locomotives that it took into its own stock, and the transferring of names between locomotives. I describe instances of both practices in some of the following picture captions.

My next visit to the LMR was with the Imperial College Railway Society on 26 April 1948. We travelled there from Waterloo via Liss and enjoyed a trip round the Hollywater Loop. My last two visits were with my father on 2 September 1950 and 5 September 1953, both Open Days. My father went alone to another Open Day on 23 May 1955.

ON
TEST
600
L M R

Opposite page WD 2-10-0 No 73651 with connecting rods and parts of the Walschaerts valve gear removed at Longmoor Downs shed, photographed during the Imperial College Railway Society visit of 26 April 1948. This locomotive was originally No 3651, later No 73651, and was built by the North British Locomotive Co in 1943, Works No 25437. It was later named *Gordon* and renumbered 600, as seen in the second photograph taken at Longmoor on 23 May 1955, with the locomotive in LMR blue livery with white-painted wheel-tyres. The name *Gordon* had originally been carried by an ex-Taff Vale Railway 0-6-2T, No 28, built in 1897, which became GWR No 450 and WD No 70205. Both locomotives have been preserved. *AND/AD*

Above A 2-8-0 and two 2-10-0s giving footplate trips at Longmoor Downs during the Open Day of 5 September 1953; the ticket price was sixpence. The locomotives are No 79250 (later No 401) *Major General McMullen*, No 73651 (later No 600) *Gordon* and No 73797 (later No 601) *Kitchener*. Note the wider firebox of the 2-10-0 design; also, the use of five, instead of four, pairs of driving wheels gave an axle loading lower than that of the 2-8-0. *AD*

Right United States Army 2-8-0, WD No 93257 (later No 700) *Carl R. Gray Jr*, built in 1944 by the American Locomotive Co (Works No 71512), at Longmoor Downs station on the Open Day of Saturday 2 September 1950. The engine is in plain black livery and, sandwiched between two others, was giving footplate rides.

Left Major General Frank S. Ross, one of the US Army 0-6-0Ts built by the Davenport Locomotive Works in 1943, on display at Longmoor on 5 September 1953. This engine was originally WD No 74382. The 'Heath Robinson' flying connections to the front dome and whistle, and the mechanical lubricator on the cylinder, do not look very sound. *AD*

Below A decrepit and numberless 'Dean Goods' 0-6-0 at Longmoor Downs on 5 September 1953. The War Department had 108 of the total of 280 of these GWR '2301' Class locomotives, numbering them from 93 to 200, and many were used overseas in both World Wars. Some were fitted with pannier tanks and condensing apparatus. No 2516 of this Class is now part of the National Collection and can be seen at the Great Western Railway Museum, Swindon.

Basingstoke

The first railway to reach Basingstoke was the London & Southampton, which opened the portion of its route from London (a terminus at Nine Elms, a mile and a half south of the present Waterloo station) to Basingstoke on 10 June 1839. The route was completed on 11 May 1840 when the portion from Basingstoke to Winchester was opened. By then the name of the company had been changed to the London & South Western Railway Company (L&SWR), so that when a proposed branch from Bishopstoke to Gosport was opened, the inhabitants of Gosport and nearby Portsmouth would not be made to feel subservient to those of Southampton!

The next railway to reach Basingstoke was the Great Western, which, on 1 November 1848, opened a 13½-mile broad gauge branch line from Southcote Junction, just west of Reading on the Hungerford line, to a new station of its own, which, incidentally, survived until 1 January 1932. The change of gauge precluded a connection between the GWR branch and the L&SWR main line. It was not until mixed gauge track from Oxford through Didcot and a new connecting curve west of Reading to Basingstoke had been completed on 22 December 1856 that a standard gauge junction could be installed and through trains run from the Midlands to stations on the South Coast.

During the 1850s and early 1860s the L&SWR completed a route from Worting Junction, a few miles beyond Basingstoke, to Exeter. Andover was reached on 3 July 1854, Salisbury on 1 May 1859 and Exeter (Queen Street) on 18 July 1860. Further penetrations into the West Country were opened right up until the end of the century.

The last railway to reach Basingstoke was the Basingstoke & Alton Light Railway, opened on 1 June 1901 soon after the Light Railways Act of 1896 had been passed. This line was closed on 1 January 1917 and the track lifted and sent overseas for use by the military during the First World War. After the war the L&SWR tried to avoid relaying the line, but failed, and it was reopened on 18 August 1924. In 1933 the company at last got permission to close the line, but before it was completely dismantled it was used at least twice by film companies. On one occasion, for the Gainsborough picture *The Wrecker*, a train was filmed running full tilt into a steam lorry on a level crossing. Its most famous use was in 1937

Maunsell Class 'S15' 4-6-0 No 30833 at the London end of Basingstoke station on Saturday 7 July 1962. The headcode indicates a train from Southampton Terminus to Waterloo.

for the making of the Will Hay film *Oh, Mr Porter!*, Cliddesden station becoming 'Buggleskelly'.

Basingstoke station was, and remains, an excellent place for railway photography because the line runs east-west and trains are thus well lit throughout the day. The line from Reading brought ex-GWR, and latterly ex-LMS, locomotives there, which greatly added to the interest.

My first visit to Basingstoke was with Derek Lee on 14 December 1944, some years before either of us had, or could have, taken up photography. The most interesting engine we saw was ex-L&SWR Adams Class 'T3' 4-4-0 No 563, built in 1893. It was withdrawn from service in 1945 but was restored to its pre-Grouping condition in 1948 and now forms part of the National Collection. We visited Basingstoke again on 11 September 1948; by then I had started taking acceptable pictures with my 'Vest Pocket Kodak' camera, and I include six pictures taken that day in the present collection.

During the 1960s my father and I visited Basingstoke together on four occasions to take photographs. He also made numerous mid-week visits on his own.

Below On the same day and standing at almost the same spot as No 30833 in the previous photograph is BR Standard Class '4' 4-6-0 No 75077. The man in front of the engine, a member of the station staff judging from his uniform, is about to secure the train number board with the dangling rope. *AD*

Right BR Standard Class '5' 4-6-0 No 73089 _Maid of Astolat_ waits for a 'clear' signal at the western end of Basingstoke station on Saturday 1 August 1964. The engine had acquired its name from 'King Arthur' Class 4-6-0 No 30744, one of the original Urie-design locomotives of the class. The signals were pneumatically operated. Note the coaling stage of the locomotive shed in the background.

73089

381

Opposite page Maunsell 'Lord Nelson' Class 4-6-0 No 851 *Sir Francis Drake* heads a Bournemouth train at Basingstoke on Saturday 11 September 1948. This picture, showing the engine in SR livery, was taken at 4.50 pm. Two minutes later a pilot, Class 'U' 2-6-0 No 1629, was attached, as shown in the second picture.

Above One of the rebuilt ex-LB&SCR Class 'L' 4-6-4Ts, No 2329 *Stephenson*, SR Class 'N15X', at the eastern end of Basingstoke station on Saturday 11 September 1948 with a train of ex-L&SWR carriages. This platform was used for trains on the line to Reading, and the starting signal is of GWR design. The engine is in SR malachite green livery.

Below A view of Basingstoke engine shed taken on Wednesday 12 April 1950 from the window of a train to Bournemouth. The nearest locomotives are Nos 30453 *King Arthur* and 31633, a 2-6-0 of Class 'U'. *King Arthur* was built by Maunsell after the Grouping of 1923, but retained the Urie-design cab of the original L&SWR engines. The engine under the hoist is a Drummond '700' Class 0-6-0 goods. *AD*

Rebuilt Bulleid 'West Country' Class 4-6-2 No 34047 *Callington* at the east end of Basingstoke station on Saturday 7 July 1962. The fireman is putting water in the tender. The second photograph shows the original appearance of locomotives of this class: 'air-smoothed' 'West Country' 'Pacific' No 34041 *Wilton* stands at Basingstoke on Saturday 1 August 1964. It was in BR lined green livery, and was bound for the Reading line on a Poole to Birkenhead express. *AND/AD*

The down 'Bournemouth Belle' is restarted by rebuilt 'Merchant Navy' Class 'Pacific' No 35014 *Nederland Line* after being stopped in Basingstoke station for examination of a hot axle box on Saturday 1 August 1964.

Above Looking now at activity on the former GWR side of the station, '6100' Class 2-6-2T No 6163, still bearing its pre-nationalisation lettering, was photographed at Basingstoke on Saturday 11 September 1948. The dirty paintwork of the carriage was not unusual in those days.

Below No 5376, a member of the Churchward '4300' Class of 2-6-0 introduced by the GWR in 1911, of which 235 members (at least) were built, stands in Basingstoke station on the same day.

Above Former Railway Operating Division (ROD) 2-8-0 No 3020 of Robinson, Great Central Railway, design but owned - before nationalisation - by the GWR, at Basingstoke, again on Saturday 11 September 1948. Former GWR engines were not renumbered by BR, so could retain their splendid brass numberplates. The chimneys of the locomotive shed are visible above the goods van in the background.

Right Independent Snowplough DB 965221 and ex-GWR 4-6-0 No 6830 *Buckenhill Grange en route* for Shrewsbury on Monday 29 March 1965. Like many others by this date, the engine has lost its cabside brass numberplate, the number being painted on in white. *AD*

Tonbridge

On 26 May 1842 was opened the first railway to Tonbridge (until May 1893 spelled Tunbridge): the line built by the South Eastern Railway (SER), which runs 19½ miles due east from a junction with the old main line to Brighton just south of Redhill station. The line was continued eastwards in stages, reaching Folkestone on 28 June 1843. Just over two years later, on 20 September 1845, a branch down to Tunbridge Wells opened, and this was extended on 1 February 1852 to St Leonards, there joining a line opened on 13 February 1851 from Ashford. The last new line to reach Tonbridge was from St John's via Sevenoaks, and shortened the distance by rail from London by some 10 miles. It was opened for passengers on 1 May 1868.

Tonbridge station, like Basingstoke, is an excellent place for watching and photographing trains because once again the platforms run from east to west and trains are well lit all day. I took pictures of steam locomotives there on four occasions, but my father did so more than a dozen times, his penultimate visit being made on 10 June 1961 two days before the introduction of electric services to the east.

A Maunsell Class 'Q' 0-6-0 goods engine on a passenger train at platform 3 of Tonbridge station on Monday 6 June 1949. My father and I had travelled in the train from Redhill. Note the 'birdcage' lookout of the leading carriage, the British Railways number in Southern numerals, and the ugly large chimney required for a multiple-jet blastpipe.

One of the six three-cylinder Maunsell 2-6-0s of Class 'N1'. The first of these engines (No 822) was completed for the SE&CR in 1922 and the others were built in 1930. The running plate extends to the front of the engine and, with the vertical plate over the buffer beam, covers the end of the inside cylinder. The larger-wheeled 'U1' (6 feet, as compared with 5 ft 6 in) 2-6-0s had a similar appearance at the front. When this picture was taken, on Saturday 7 May 1960, the lines through the station had been electrified and the down through line relaid with flat-bottomed rail. *AD*

Right 'Schools' Class 4-4-0 No 30902 *Wellington* on an up train at the west end of Tonbridge station on Monday 6 June 1949. The engine bears the Hastings line headcode and the train is standing in the through platform, No 1, which was formed from a bay platform in 1935.

247
401

Above A former LB&SCR 2-6-0 of Billinton design, SR Class 'K', at the London end of platform 2 of Tonbridge station on Saturday 26 June 1948. The engine still carries its Southern number in yellow characters with green shading.

Below Class 'I3' 4-4-2T No 32082 in platform 2 on Monday 6 June 1949. In November 1909 superheated members of this Marsh LB&SCR design, Nos 23 and 26, were compared with the LNWR unsuperheated 'Precursor' Class 4-4-0 No 7 *Titan* (LMS No 5276) in working the 'Sunny South Express' and proved the better design, regularly running 90 miles between Rugby and Croydon without taking water. The lettering is in SR-style transfers and unusually the engine has retained its buffer-beam number after receiving its smokebox numberplate.

Above A down freight train, hauled by No 31716, one of the Southern Railway's most numerous class of engine, the ex-SE&CR Wainwright 0-6-0 of Class 'C', of which 109 were built between 1900 and 1908, runs through Tonbridge station on Monday 1 December 1954. In fact, the Southern had 108 because No 685 was converted to a saddle tank of Class 'S' in 1917. 'Schools' Class 4-4-0 No 921 *Shrewsbury* is in the background, standing in the bay platform. *AD*

Below Wainwright Class 'H' 0-4-4T No 31503, built in 1905, in lined British Railways black livery. It was photographed on 6 June 1949.

No 1748, an elegant Wainwright Class 'D' 4-4-0 built in 1903 for the SE&CR, stands at the east end of platform 3 of Tonbridge station on 6 June 1949. No 737 of this Class belongs to the National Railway Museum. The 'colour light' starting signals, immediately in front of the locomotive's smokebox, are interesting, and were produced by removing the arms from conventional semaphore signals to leave just the spectacle plates; also of note is the guard's 'birdcage' look-out of the SE&CR first coach.

A Maunsell rebuild of a Wainwright Class 'D' 4-4-0, Class 'D1' No 31470, photographed on 17 March 1958. The rebuilding was carried out at Ashford Works in 1926, and the locomotive is in the final form of the British Railways lined black livery. *AD*

Wainwright Class 'E' 4-4-0 No 275 (when built in 1906) on 6 June 1949. The wording 'Southern' is just visible through the dirt on the tender, and the British Railways number is in Southern Railway transfers. The fireman seems to be wielding a long fire-iron.

This picture of Wainwright 'E' Class 4-4-0 after rebuilding by Maunsell to Class 'El' may be compared with the picture of 'D1' class No 31470 opposite. The only difference is that the coupling rods of the 'E1' are fluted and those of the 'D1' are flat. I had to refer to Mr Burtt's book to discover this! *AD*

The handsome 'L' Class 4-4-0s were to a design started by Wainwright but completed by Maunsell. No 31767, one of 12 built by Beyer, Peacock & Co of Manchester during 1914, is shown in SR-style lined malachite green livery on 18 April 1953. *AD*

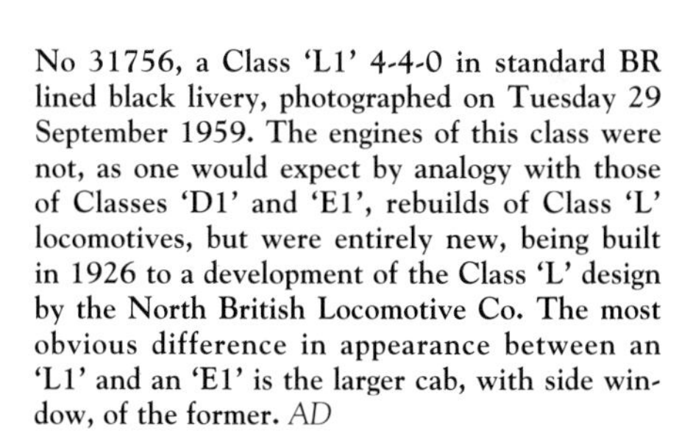

No 31756, a Class 'L1' 4-4-0 in standard BR lined black livery, photographed on Tuesday 29 September 1959. The engines of this class were not, as one would expect by analogy with those of Classes 'D1' and 'E1', rebuilds of Class 'L' locomotives, but were entirely new, being built in 1926 to a development of the Class 'L' design by the North British Locomotive Co. The most obvious difference in appearance between an 'L1' and an 'E1' is the larger cab, with side window, of the former. *AD*

British Railways Standard 'Britannia' Class '7P6F' 'Pacific' No 70004 *William Shakespeare* passes Tonbridge on the 'Golden Arrow' of Monday 17 March 1958. Note the headboard, flags, and golden arrows on the smoke deflectors. This locomotive was exhibited on the South Bank, London, during the Festival of Britain in 1951. *AD*

Because Beyer, Peacock & Co could supply only 12 of the 22 'L' Class locomotives needed for the summer traffic of 1914, and because no other British builder could supply the remainder, the Berlin firm of A. Borsig built the last 10 locomotives, BR Nos 31772 to 31781. They went into traffic in August 1914, on the 5th of which month the British entered the First World War. No 31778 is seen in lined BR black livery on 17 March 1958. *AD*

Bournemouth

The first railway in the neighbourhood of Bournemouth was the Southampton & Dorchester Railway, opened on 1 June 1847, which ran from a junction with the L&SWR just north of the Southampton terminus through Brockenhurst, Ringwood and Wimborne to Hamworthy Junction and thence through Wareham to Dorchester. A 2-mile branch line from Hamworthy Junction brought passengers to the original station at Poole, from which they could travel by omnibus 5 miles eastwards to Bournemouth.

It was not until 1870 that a railway was opened to Bournemouth itself. A line from Ringwood to Christchurch, 7 miles to the south, was opened on 13 November 1860, and this was extended 4½ miles eastwards to a terminus in Bournemouth on 14 March 1870. It was the opening of the Bournemouth Direct Railway, on 5 March 1888, between Brockenhurst and Christchurch that completed the present main line from Waterloo to Bournemouth. The link from Ringwood to Bournemouth then ceased to be of primary importance, and was closed on 30 September 1935.

Part of a route that eventually linked Bournemouth with Burnham-on-Sea, on the Bristol Channel, and also with Bath and Bristol, was opened on 31 October 1860 by the Dorset Central Railway. It was a line from Blandford to a junction with the Southampton & Dorchester Railway south of, and facing, Wimborne station. In 1862 the Dorset Central amalgamated with the Somerset Central Railway, whose line ran from Burnham-on-Sea to Bruton, on the Great Western line to Taunton, to form the Somerset & Dorset Railway. The new company linked its two lines on 31 August 1863 and ran trains to the original Poole station, these having to reverse at Wimborne.

In 1872 the L&SWR opened a line from Poole New Junction (now called Broadstone), about 3 miles south of Wimborne, down to a new station at Poole, just over half a mile to the north-west of the old. Passenger traffic at the old station ceased in 1893, and the station was thereafter used only for goods, being renamed Hamworthy Goods.

On 15 June 1874 the Poole & Bournemouth Railway opened a line from the new Poole station eastwards to a new terminus in Bournemouth - Bournemouth West. This line enabled Somerset & Dorset Railway trains to run from Burnham-on-Sea to Bournemouth. Trains could also run from Bath and Bristol when the Somerset & Dorset Joint Railway (S&DJR) was opened between there and Evercreech Junction in 1875. The Midland Railway used that route for services between the North of England and Bournemouth, which continued, under successive owners, until the line was closed on 7 March 1966. These services included the 'Pines Express', named in 1927, between Manchester and Bournemouth West.

Originally, S&D trains reversed at Wimborne on their way to the coast, but a connecting curve to Broadstone was opened on 14 December 1885 and allowed through running. In 1893 two further connecting curves were opened to eliminate the need for train reversals. The first, opened on 18 May, linked Poole with Hamworthy Junction and allowed through running between Bournemouth West and Wareham; the second, opened on 1 June, allowed through running between Bournemouth Central and the stations on the line out of Bournemouth West.

My experience of the Bournemouth railway scene in the steam era was during a family holiday in 1949. We travelled from Waterloo in the 'Bournemouth Belle'; this Pullman train first ran in July 1931, was withdrawn during the Second World War, and was reinstated in 1946. The 1947 timetable showed the train leaving Waterloo at 12.30 pm and reaching Bournemouth West, the end of its journey, at 2.47 pm. The train formation on the day of our journey, 13 April, starting from the rear and using the car letters employed for seat reservations, was as follows: 'A' - TC No 94; 'B' - Car No 45; 'C' - 3rd Class Car No 7; 'D' - 3rd Class Car No 31; 'E' - TC No 294; 'F' - 3rd Class Car No ?; 'G' - 'Sunbeam'; 'E' - 'Glencoe'; 'J' - 'Orpheus'; 'K' - 'Portia'; 'L' - TC No 96; and 'M' - 3rd Class Car No 41. The train locomotive was 'Merchant Navy' Class 4-6-2 No 35011 *General Steam Navigation* - air-smoothed in those days.

The hotel at which we stayed was close to Bournemouth West station and we travelled by train quite frequently during the holiday, visiting Christchurch, Wimborne and, on the branch line from Wareham to Swanage (opened on 20 May 1885), Corfe Castle. My parents stayed at Bournemouth on three later occasions during 1950 and 1951, and I include two pictures taken in 1950.

On 10 July 1967 electric trains took over the Waterloo to Bournemouth Central service and main-line steam ended on the Southern Region.

Below The 'Bournemouth Belle' at Bournemouth West on Wednesday 13 April 1949 at the end of our journey from Waterloo. The locomotive is 'Merchant Navy' Class 'Pacific' No 35011 *General Steam Navigation*. The pivoted metal strips (treadles) against the running rails further from the platforms were depressed by the wheel flanges of a locomotive or vehicle at the end of the platforms, and worked indicators in the signal box.

Right 'Schools' Class No 30936 *Cranleigh* at the east end of Southampton Central station on Thursday 14 April 1949 on a train for Waterloo. Note the two shunt signals - the shorter arms, each bearing a letter 'S' - at the bottom of the signal bracket posts. The locomotive is newly painted in BR lined black livery.

30936

'Lord Nelson' Class No 30861 *Lord Anson* on a Waterloo express stands beneath the same signals on Saturday 16 April 1949.
The locomotive and train are in Southern malachite green with yellow and black lettering and lining. The fireman is busy putting more water into the tender.

Also beautifully repainted in Southern malachite green, Class 'N15X' 4-6-0 No 32333 *Remembrance* leaves Bournemouth Central on a London train. This and its sister locomotives were rebuilds of the seven Class 'L' 4-6-4Ts designed by L. Billinton for the LB&SCR and built between 1914 and 1922. Maunsell rebuilt the locomotives to the form shown between 1934 and 1936. The memorial plaque from the side tank of the original engine can be seen on the central splasher; it read 'In grateful remembrance of 532 men of the LB&SC Rly who gave their lives for their country, 1914-1919'.

A former L&SWR Drummond 'T9' 4-4-0 with its British Railways number 30707, and tender lettering applied using Southern Railway-style transfers, photographed at Bournemouth West on Saturday 16 April 1949. The driver and fireman are putting water in the tender, and near the water cranes are two barrows that porters will use for transporting passengers' luggage. The 'T9' Class locomotives were nicknamed 'Greyhounds'; in the 1920s they were fitted with superheaters, extended smokeboxes and stovepipe chimneys. Visually they could be divided into two categories: the engines with coupling rod splashers and inside-frame eight-wheel tenders, as shown in this picture, and the engines with wider cabs and splashers that could accommodate the coupling rods, as shown in the picture of No 336 on the next page.

43194
43194

Left Class 'T9' 4-4-0 No 336 in SR livery on a train of early L&SWR stock at Bournemouth Central on 14 April 1949. This locomotive, with its wider cab and splashers and outside-frame tender, may be compared with No 30707 in the photograph on page 69.

Below left One of the 0-6-0 goods engines, LMS Class '3F', built to the Johnson Midland Railway design for the S&DJR in 1896. The shed code 22D indicates allocation to Templecombe motive power depot. No 43194 was photographed at Bournemouth West on 12 April 1950 on a train of former Southern Railway carriages. *AD*

Above A Fowler 0-6-0 goods, LMS Class '4F', built in 1922 for the S&DJR (No 60) at Bournemouth West, also in April 1950. The engine, in early British Railways livery, was from Bath shed (22C). *AD*

Right Class 'H15' two-cylinder 4-6-0 No 483, designed by Urie for the L&SWR and built at Eastleigh in 1914, stands at the east end of Bournemouth locomotive yard on Thursday 14 April 1949. The high-capacity tender, carrying 7 tons of coal and 5,200 gallons of water, was desirable for a line having no water troughs.

Above Former LB&SCR Stroudley 0-6-0T, Class 'E1', No 2112 standing just beyond the turntable at Bournemouth shed on 16 April 1949. This engine was built at Brighton in 1877 and originally bore the number 112 and name *Versailles*. It was 'dead' when this picture was taken, but would have been used as shed pilot for moving locomotives and wagons at the depot.

Below Photographed on 18 April 1949, during a visit to the shed, was 'S11' Class 4-4-0 No 398. Notice the elegant chimney. The unsightly white streaks down the smokebox were due to priming, the precipitation of chemicals from the boiler feed water.

Above right Drummond Class 'M7' 0-4-4T No 30028, built for the L&SWR in 1904, in the then new lined black BR livery and fitted with a smokebox numberplate, is on a push-pull train bound for Swanage at Corfe Castle station on Saturday 16 April 1949. The train is waiting to allow the Swanage-Wareham train to pass, the branch being single line. That train was worked by another 'M7', No 52, still in Southern black livery. The modern concrete and enamelled steel station sign is rather at odds with the period signal box.

Right A view from the Corfe Castle mound of No 30028 hauling its push-pull train back to Wareham later in the day on 16 April 1949. Note the unbelievable - these days - almost complete absence of cars!

CORFE
30028
30028

2. Main lines

East Coast Main Line in Hertfordshire

A Bill for the construction of a railway from London to York was passed in 1846, and on 7 August 1850 the Great Northern Railway (GNR) was opened from a temporary London terminus, at Maiden Lane, to Doncaster. A few miles north of Peterborough the line ran north-north-east to Boston, then north-west through Lincoln to Doncaster. It was in 1852 that the direct line from Peterborough, through Grantham, to Doncaster was opened. Later that year, on 14 October, King's Cross station, the fifth of the surviving London termini to be built, opened.

My father had a number of railway enthusiast friends with whom he went on railway expeditions, and one of them had a special knowledge of signalling and had the entrée to a number of signal boxes on the King's Cross main line, including Greenwood, to the south of Hadley South Tunnel, and Wood Green. My father was therefore enabled to take photographs from and in the vicinity of those boxes. His visits to the line covered the period from 1952 to 1961. It was within that period, between 1953 and 1959, that the tracks between Greenwood and Potters Bar were quadrupled, new double-track tunnels being built beside the existing tunnels at Hadley South, Hadley North and Potters Bar, and the station at Potters Bar being largely rebuilt.

Above right Greenwood signal box, with signalman Sellers at the window, photographed on 26 April 1952. The brickwork around the lower part of the box would have been built to protect the interlocking and other mechanisms from bomb damage during Second World War air raids. *AD*

Below right Signalman Sellers inside the box on the same day. Heating during cold weather was by the solid fuel cooking range in the fireplace on the left of the picture. An interesting array of block signalling instruments is on the shelf over the signal and point levers. *AD*

Below Gresley Class 'N2' 0-6-2Ts Nos 69524 and 69549 on trains of suburban stock near Wood Green No 1 signal box on Friday 27 July 1956. The varnished teak of many of the carriages in the background has been covered with the cream and red paint of that era, while the upper quadrant arms of the large signal gantry would originally have been the centrally pivoted arms of the GNR 'somersault' signals. *AD*

GREENWOOD

Peppercorn Class 'A1' 4-6-2 No 60139 *Sea Eagle* hauls an up express out of Hadley South Tunnel on 26 April 1952. My father took the photograph from Greenwood signal box. The carriages of the train are in the red and cream livery of the period. *AD*

Above Thompson Class 'L1' 2-6-4T No 67745 brings a train of decidedly mixed rolling-stock past Greenwood box on 26 April 1952. One hundred of these two-cylinder tank locomotives were built, the first appearing in 1945. *AD*

Below Thompson Class 'B1' 4-6-0 No 61251 *Oliver Bury* hauling an up goods train out of Hadley South Tunnel on the same day. The shed code on the smokebox door is 34A, King's Cross, and the letters SC beneath it stand for 'self-cleaning', a type of smokebox fitted with internal wire mesh screens to prevent ashes collecting at the bottom and allow them to be ejected through the chimney by the exhaust. *AD*

Travelling towards the tunnel on the same day is Class 'N2' 0-6-2T No 69584 with a train of articulated suburban stock. In an articulated unit the ends of each adjacent pair of carriages are carried by a common bogie. Thus a 'quint' (five-carriage) unit has only six bogies, instead of the ten required for separate carriages, a considerable saving in weight. The 'N2' engines were of a Gresley GNR design and first appeared in January 1921. After the 1923 Grouping, the LNER increased the number of locomotives in the Class from 60 to 147. Many, like the one shown in the picture, were fitted with condensing apparatus for working in the tunnels of the Metropolitan Line. *AD*

Gresley 'A4' 'Pacific' No 60029 *Woodcock* on the up 'Flying Scotsman' leaving Welwyn North Tunnel on Wednesday 28 April 1954. The carriages are in the BR red and cream livery. Six locomotives of this Class have been preserved, including No 60022 *Mallard*, which gained the unbroken world speed record for a steam locomotive of 126.4 mph in 1938. *AD*

Midland Main Lines

My parents came from Derbyshire and almost all the train journeys of my childhood started from St Pancras. In visiting my father's parents and other members of his family, the destination was Derby; in visiting my mother's parents the destination was Ambergate at first, but later Bakewell. For country holidays at Appleby, on the Settle-Carlisle line, and for the seaside at Ayr and Scarborough (the latter visited via Derby), we travelled along more former Midland Railway main lines. These were the lines that my father and I came to know, and like, best.

Right Elstree was a Sunday morning cycle ride from where I was living at Stanmore. Stanier '8F' 2-8-0 No 48181 hauls a goods train out of the southern portal of Elstree New Tunnel on 22 February 1953. On that day the parallel tunnel of the fast lines was closed and all traffic was using the goods lines.

Below Fowler '4F' 0-6-0 No 44556 hauls a freight train on the down fast line beyond Elstree on Monday 27 September 1954. The Midland line from Bedford to London was opened in 1867, St Pancras station opening the following year. *AD*

Ex-LMS Fowler Compound 4-4-0 No 41048, built in 1924 and withdrawn in 1957, hauls a train of red and cream-liveried carriages on the down slow line beyond Elstree station on 27 September 1954. The hill through which the twin Elstree tunnels pass is visible in the distance. *AD*

Above On the same day an up suburban train approaches Elstree hauled by British Railways Standard Class '4' 2-6-4T No 80060. The tall signals were to provide good visibility beyond the overbridges near which this picture was taken; the lower arms were for viewing by the crew of a train stopped at the signal. *AD*

Below Stanier 'Black Five' No 45289 takes a train of condemned tube 'Standard' stock on the down goods line through the remains of Oakley station, Bedfordshire, closed on 15 September 1958; my father took this photograph on 9 April 1964. The ex-Midland Railway signal on the up goods line, and the guard enjoying the ride in his brake-van, are worthy of notice. *AD*

Above A Bradford to Bristol express approaches Breadsall crossing, some 2½ miles north of Derby, behind Class '5' 4-6-0 No 44849 on Friday 16 May 1958. One former Midland Railway signal remains, in the distance. *AD*

Below Hughes 'Crab' 2-6-0 No 42887 emerges from Headstones Tunnel, just south of the Monsal Dale viaduct, on Thursday 21 September 1950. Although the line from Ambergate to Rowsley was opened in 1849, it was not until 1867 that the Midland Railway completed its route to Manchester. The stations on the line were closed 100 years later and trains no longer ran between Matlock and Chinley North Junction after 1 July 1968. *AD*

Stanier 'Jubilee' Class 4-6-0 No 45655 *Keith* takes an up express from Manchester out of Milford Tunnel, 855 yards long, between Belper and Duffield, on Saturday 23 July 1955. The signal posts suspended from the gantry brought the signals as low as possible so as to be visible from well within the tunnel. It is interesting to note that the telegraph wires are carried over the hill. *AD*

On Monday 20 April 1953 a Manchester to St Pancras express, hauled by a clean 'Jubilee' Class 4-6-0, passes the point south of Cromford where the A6 road, Cromford Canal, railway and river Derwent are close together. *AD*

Above On Wednesday 31 May 1950 a Class '5' 4-6-0 takes its train towards Peak Forest Junction and Manchester past the Buxton Central Lime Works. The cottages stand inside a triangle junction; the Miller's Dale to Buxton line passes behind the spot from which my father took this picture. *AD*

Below An up freight train on the Settle-Carlisle line near Crosby Garrett, between Kirkby Stephen and Appleby, photographed on Saturday 4 September 1954. The locomotive is a Class '4F' 0-6-0 goods. *AD*

Great Western in Berkshire

The Great Western Railway - so named even before it was built - obtained an Act of Parliament for building a line from London to Bristol in 1835. The first portion, from Bishops Road (Paddington) to Taplow, was opened on 4 June 1838, but it was not until 30 June 1841 that the whole line came into use. Nine months' delay had been caused by difficulties encountered during construction of Box Tunnel, a few miles east of Bath and almost 2 miles long.

Brunel's line to Bristol was laid out for speed. For 70 of its 118 miles the ruling gradient is less than 1 in 1000. The worst gradient is the 3 miles at 1 in 100 of the section including Box Tunnel.

Important dates in the history of the line are 16 January 1854, when the departure side of the new Paddington terminus was opened; 1 October 1861, when mixed gauge track reached Paddington from Reading West Junction; and 21 May 1892, when the last broad gauge train arrived at Paddington.

Above A down goods in Sonning cutting on Tuesday 31 March 1953 hauled by '6100' Class 2-6-2T No 6130. This famous cutting is almost 2 miles long and varies in depth between 20 and 50 feet. Work on it started in the spring of 1836, and after more than one contractor had failed, Brunel took charge and completed it by the end of 1839. The bridge in the picture replaced a timber structure in 1893 when the cutting was enlarged and two more lines laid through it. *AD*

Left A down local train with five vans attached to the rear near Purley on the same day. The locomotive is 'Modified Hall' '6959' Class No 7900 *Saint Peter's Hall*. *AD*

Above A down goods train including, next to the engine, five loaded cattle trucks, near Purley - between Reading and Pangbourne - on 31 March 1953. The locomotive is Collett '2251' Class 0-6-0 No 2264. Notice the telegraph poles, a usual part of the steam railway scene, and the typical GWR lower quadrant semaphore signals. *AD*

Below An up loose-coupled goods train near Twyford on Wednesday 28 April 1954 hauled by one of the 863 members of Collett's '5700' Class 0-6-0PT, No 3622, built at Swindon in 1939. *AD*

One of the later '4300' Class 2-6-0s, with side-window cab, hauls a down goods train near Purley on 31 March 1953.
All the wagons are wooden-bodied and some bear vestiges of the names of former owners. *AD*

Above One of the Collett 2-8-0s of the '2800' Class, No 3832, on an up freight train passing Iver station on Friday 16 October 1959. These engines differed from those of the 1903 Churchward design by having side-window cabs. The second wagon of the train carries a container that would have started and finished its journey by road. *AD*

Below British Railways Standard 'Britannia' Class 'Pacific' No 70027 *Rising Star* on a down express near Iver on the same day. The large reporting number on the smokebox door indicates that the train is the 5.50 pm Paddington to Swansea. *AD*

South Western from Waterloo

This section of the book is a supplement to the sections on Basingstoke and Bournemouth, and shows Southern Region steam trains in action between stations.

Below Unrebuilt 'Merchant Navy' 4-6-2 No 35006 *Peninsular & Oriental S. N. Co* on a down train of milk tank wagons approaching Esher on Saturday 9 April 1949. The locomotive is in the original yellow-lined malachite green livery, but with British Railways number and tender lettering. Note the semaphore signals in the distance - colour light signalling had not yet been installed.

Bottom 'West Country' Class 'Pacific' No 34032 *Camelford*, in malachite green livery, produces a satisfying display of smoke as it approaches Esher on 9 April 1949 on a Plymouth train.

Above No 30755, the last-built of the Urie Class 'N15' 4-6-0s, completed just after the Grouping in March 1923, was named *The Red Knight* in 1925 and was one of five 'King Arthurs' to be fitted with a multiple-jet blastpipe and large-diameter chimney. It is seen near Winchfield station on a train from Southampton Terminus on Wednesday 12 September 1956, and carries the BR lined green livery; the Bulleid carriages are in malachite green. *AD*

Below Urie ex-L&SWR 4-6-0 Class 'S15' on a decidedly mixed goods train at Worting on Monday 23 May 1955. The headcode suggests that it has come from the main line to Southampton. The telegraph poles carry an unusually large number of wires. *AD*

Above Rebuilt 'Merchant Navy' 4-6-2 No 35004 *Cunard White Star* brings a train from Bournemouth off the line from Worting Junction flyover on to the up fast line at Worting Junction signal box on Monday 29 March 1965. The rear of a train for the Southampton line is visible in the distance. *AD*

Below A permanent way train including six bogie hopper wagons for ballast, with side delivery chutes, photographed from Worting Junction signal box on 13 May 1957. The locomotive is 'King Arthur' 'N15' Class 4-6-0 No 30450 *Sir Kay*, built in 1925 at Eastleigh. *AD*

Above right My father enjoyed the privilege of a photographic pass for Southern Region non-electrified lines and was able to obtain better pictures at Worting Junction than most enthusiasts. This photograph shows an up train from Salisbury hauled by 'S15' Class 4-6-0 No 30827 in clean black livery on 29 March 1965. *AD*

Below right A down Plymouth train passes beneath the flyover hauled by 'Lord Nelson' Class 4-6-0 No 30863 *Lord Rodney* on Monday 13 May 1957. *AD*

30827
435

251

3. Branch lines

Wensleydale

In 1950 we spent the first week of our family summer holiday at Hawes in Wensleydale. The dale is named after a village near its entrance, not after the river that flows along it, which is the Ure. We chose Hawes both as a centre for walking in the northern countryside, which we loved so much, and as a place from which we could visit by train the Aysgarth falls and the castles of Bolton and Middleham.

The railway through Hawes was the Wensleydale branch. This was really two branch lines, one running west from Northallerton on the East Coast Main Line and the other running east from Garsdale on the Settle-Carlisle line, which met end-on at Hawes. The branch from Northallerton was built in stages, the dates of opening for passenger services being: Northallerton to Leeming Bar (5¾ miles), 6 March 1848; Leeming Bar to Bedale (1¾ miles), 1 February 1855; Bedale to Leyburn (10 miles), 19 May 1856; Leyburn to Askrigg (12 miles), 1 June 1878; and Askrigg to Hawes (4¼ miles), 1 October 1878. From 31 July 1854 the branch belonged to the North Eastern Railway (NER).

The branch from Garsdale, originally called Hawes Junction, was built by the Midland Railway and opened on 1 October 1878. It was 5¾ miles long, so the distance by rail from Northallerton to Garsdale was 39¾ miles.

At the Grouping of 1923, the line from Northallerton to Hawes became part of the LNER and the continuation to Garsdale part of the LMS. At nationalisation, these sections of line passed to the North Eastern and London Midland Regions respectively. Passenger services between Northallerton and Hawes were withdrawn on 26 April 1954, and the last train along the whole route ran from Garsdale on Saturday 24 April. The final return journey between Garsdale and Hawes was made on Saturday 14 March 1959.

In May 1990 the Wensleydale Railway Association was constituted at a meeting in Redmire with the aim of reinstating part, or possibly all, of the Northallerton-Garsdale line. Let us hope that it achieves some degree of success.

Class 'G5' 0-4-4T No 67346 at Garsdale on Saturday 1 July 1950; it is approaching the carriages of the train in which we completed our journey to Hawes. In the distance, just beyond Moorcock (or Dandry Mire) viaduct, the train on which we had travelled from Hellifield - hauled by Class '5' 4-6-0 No 44900 - is crossing the bridge over the road (A684) from Hawes to Sedbergh. The starting signals are of typical MR design.

On a later holiday, in 1954, my father and I stayed at Appleby, and on Tuesday 7 September went by train to Garsdale whence we walked along Mallerstang to Kirkby Stephen. This picture at Garsdale station shows our train about to continue its journey to Leeds behind a dirty Stanier Class '5' 4-6-0. The ex-LMS carriage is in the attractive BR red and cream livery. The oil lamps for lighting the platform are a period feature.

Above A distant view of the 8.56 am to Hawes taken on Thursday 6 July 1950 and giving some idea of the beautiful scenery of upper Wensleydale. The locomotive is No 67324.

Below The author talking to one of the crew of Class '4F' 0-6-0 No 44197 at Hawes on 5 July 1950. Note the tender cab, which would have made travelling tender-first more bearable in a bitter northern winter. The London Midland Region 'Bonnyface' train is in the background. *AD*

Ivatt Class '2' 2-6-2T No 1206 on the 4.25 pm train for Hellifield in Hawes station on Wednesday 5 July 1950. This train was given - for reasons nobody seems to know - the nickname 'Bonnyface'. The North Eastern Region train in the far platform is the 4.00 pm for Northallerton.

Just east of Hawes station, on Thursday 6 July 1950, Class 'J25' 0-6-0 No E5645 runs round its train, in the goods yard behind the photographer, prior to its departure for Northallerton. This locomotive was of W. Worsdell's 1898 design for the NER, Class 'P1', and until the LNER renumbering of 1946 carried the number 1961. The new number 5645 was prefixed by the letter 'E' immediately after the 1948 nationalisation and would subsequently be changed to 65645.

Former NER Worsdell 1894-design Class 'O' 0-4-4T, LNER Class 'G5', No 67344 leaving Hawes on the 8.56 train to Garsdale on Wednesday 3 May 1950.
The ex-NER composite carriage with guard's lookouts and clerestory roof forms a splendid conclusion to the train.

Above Class 'G5' tank No 67324 hurries away from Hawes on the 8.56 am to Garsdale on Friday 7 July 1950. Note the van attached to the rear of the train.

Below The same locomotive at Redmire station on the 4.23 pm train to Northallerton on 5 July 1950, photographed while we waited for our train back to Hawes.

Above Characteristic NER slotted-post signals and warning sign at Redmire station on Wednesday 5 July 1950, photographed during our visit to Bolton Castle. The top of the castle towers are just visible above the wall to the right of the signal post. The finial of the latter has lost its spike.

Above right Another typical NER signal with its wooden arm working in a slotted post, photographed just west of Redmire station on the same day during our walk from the station to Bolton Castle.

Below The 5.04 pm train for Garsdale entering Leyburn station on Monday 3 July 1950. On this day we were returning to Hawes after visiting Middleham Castle. The small locomotive shed would have housed the Class 'Y3' shunting engine shown in the next picture. *AD*

Sentinel Class 'Y3' 0-4-0 shunting engine attaching four milk tank wagons to the end of the 4.38 pm train to Northallerton in Leyburn station on 3 July 1950. This station had an unusual layout - the platforms were staggered and a level crossing connected their adjacent ends. The platform for Northallerton trains was to the west of the level crossing and faced a third platform at a siding south of the running lines, used for goods.

Uttoxeter to Buxton

The route from Uttoxeter to Buxton comprised three sections of line. The first, from Uttoxeter to Rocester, was part of the North Staffordshire Railway (NSR) line from North Rode to Uttoxeter, opened in July 1849. The second, also built by the NSR, was originally a branch from Rocester to Ashbourne, and opened on 31 May 1852. The third, from Ashbourne to Buxton, was built by the London & North Western Railway (LNWR) and opened on 4 August 1899 (the date for the opening of the southernmost portion from Parsley Hay to Ashbourne). The line from Buxton had reached Hindlow, where it joined the Cromford & High Peak Railway (C&HPR), on 27 June 1892, and was opened to Parsley Hay, using a realigned and doubled section of the C&HPR, on 1 June 1894. The C&HPR had been leased to the LNWR since 1861 and was the famous mineral line that included, between Cromford and Parsley Hay, two cable-worked inclines and the Hopton Incline, which, with its maximum gradient of 1 in 14, was the steepest length of track in the United Kingdom worked by adhesion locomotives.

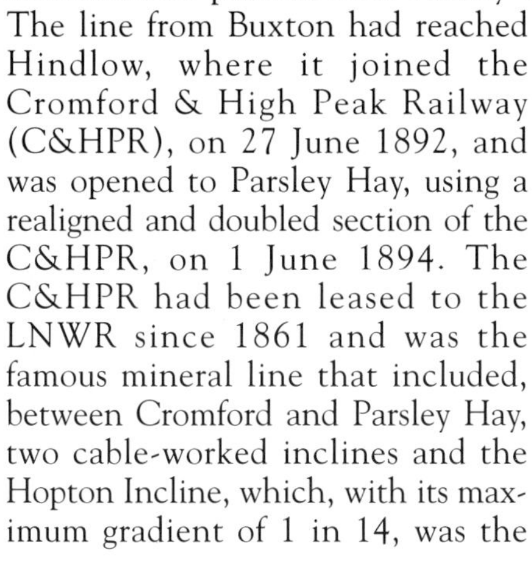

In October 1954, during a visit by my parents to members of the family who lived in Duffield, my father travelled the whole of the Uttoxeter to Ashbourne line. I saw steam trains on the line only twice: at Tissington in May 1958 and at Alsop-en-le-Dale in September 1962.

Normal passenger services were withdrawn between Uttoxeter and Buxton on 1 November 1954. For a time the line was used for goods and excursion trains, but it was completely closed on 1 June 1964. The trackbed from Ashbourne to Hartington has since been converted into the Tissington Trail.

One of the very few railway photographs my father took before the Second World War shows 2-6-4T No 2348 in Ashbourne station. The middle poster is advertising at 1 shilling the Summer Number of *Punch*, the humorous magazine that expired only a few years ago. *AD*

Above On Wednesday 20 October 1954, less than a month before the withdrawal of the service, my father travelled to Buxton on the train for Ashbourne behind Fowler Class '4P' 2-6-4T No 42365. Here is a view from the train at Clifton for Mayfield station, 10¼ miles from Uttoxeter. The ex-LNWR 0-8-0 goods locomotive has the slightly tapered form of chimney that replaced the original type. *AD*

Left Another view from the train, taken as it was about to leave the northern end of 390-yard Ashbourne Tunnel. *AD*

Above A southbound goods train at Alsop-en-le-Dale station on 27 September 1962 headed by Fowler Class '4F' 0-6-0 No 44497 from Buxton shed (9D). The station is still in good condition even though not regularly used by passenger trains for almost eight years.

Below Trains about to pass at Alsop-en-le-Dale on 20 October 1954. That on the right is the one on which my father was travelling to Buxton, the engine being No 42365. The train arriving is hauled by 2-6-4T No 42665, one of the later Stanier locomotives. The characteristic corrugated metal arm of the LNWR starting signal, mounted near the top of the post, reveals the pre-Grouping ownership of the line. *AD*

My father's train leaving Hindlow, the last but one station before Buxton, 18¾ miles from Ashbourne; the mileage to Buxton was 22½. The water pipes fed directly by the water tower are an unusual feature. It is hard to decide whether the group of men in the goods yard are about to maintain the pair of points or have gathered for a more social reason. The smoking chimneys are almost certainly those of the lime kilns fed by the limestone quarry in the background. *AD*

Hatfield to Dunstable and Leighton Buzzard

The line from Hatfield to Leighton Buzzard consisted of two branch lines with an end-on connection at Dunstable North. The first was the LNWR branch from Leighton to Dunstable, which opened on 1 June 1848 and ended 5 miles west of Luton. When, on 7 August 1850, the GNR opened its main line to London, the route lay almost 10 miles east of Luton. That important manufacturing town thus found itself isolated from the growing network of railways.

In 1855 an Act of Parliament was obtained for building a branch line - the second of the two mentioned above - from Welwyn Junction, 2½ miles north of Hatfield on the GNR main line, through Luton to Dunstable. For a time it was planned to connect the new line with a branch to be built eastwards from Welwyn to Hertford, which would have enabled trains from Luton to reach London via Hertford on the Eastern Counties Railway. However, the GNR wanted those trains to use its own main line and imposed such severe conditions about the building and structure of the bridge across that line needed for connecting the branches on either side that the plan was dropped. The Welwyn to Hertford line opened at the end of February 1858 and the Welwyn to Dunstable line was completed on 1 September 1860. The section from Luton to Dunstable had opened earlier for goods traffic on 5 April and for passengers on 3 May 1858.

Today Luton is only served by trains running on the Midland Main Line from St Pancras to Leicester and beyond. This route was not opened until 7 September 1867, prior to which MR trains from Leicester to London travelled through Bedford to Hitchin and completed their journeys over the GNR main line. It was the delays that these trains experienced on that final stage of their journeys which prompted the Midland to build its own line into London.

From Luton Hoo to Luton, the Hatfield-Dunstable line ran for more than 3 miles close to the main line from St Pancras. During my many childhood journeys to the North, I looked at the charming single-line branch hoping to see an LNER train, but I cannot remember doing so.

From 1951 until 1962 I lived at Belmont on the Stanmore Village branch. On Saturday 11 July 1953 I took myself on a circular tour with the following stages: Belmont to Harrow & Wealdstone (1 mile); Harrow & Wealdstone to Watford Junction (6½ miles); Watford Junction to St Albans (Abbey) (6½ miles); St Albans (City) to Luton (10¼ miles); Luton (Bute Street) to Dunstable North (5¼ miles); Dunstable North to Leighton Buzzard (7¼ miles); Leighton Buzzard to Watford Junction (22½ miles); and back to Belmont (7½ miles) - a total of 66¾ miles. What I missed was, of course, the 15-mile Hatfield-Luton portion of the branch.

My father travelled the complete Hatfield-Leighton Buzzard line on two occasions. The first was on Tuesday 26 July 1955 when, thanks to an influential enthusiast friend, he was able to make the return journey by goods train. The second was on Sunday 9 August 1959 when he was a passenger on the RCTS 'Grafton Tour', which ran from King's Cross through Hitchin, Bedford and Banbury to Leamington Spa, and then back to King's Cross via Daventry, Blisworth and the Leighton Buzzard to Hatfield line.

A train hauled by an 'N7' 0-6-2T enters Luton (Bute Street) station on Saturday 11 July 1953. The underhung signal is an interesting feature. Class 'N7/4' 0-6-2T No 69617, on a Dunstable train, was originally No 995, one of a batch of ten engines built at the Stratford Works of the Great Eastern Railway and completed just after the Grouping in 1923. It became LNER No 7995 and was rebuilt with a round-top firebox (Class 'N7/4') at some time after 1940. In the 1946 renumbering it became No 9617.

Former LNWR 2-4-2T of Webb's 1890 design, LMS Class '1P' No 46601 at Dunstable North on my train for Leighton Buzzard on the same day. It was allocated to Bletchley shed. The last locomotive of this class was withdrawn in 1955. On the right is a carriage of a train back to Hatfield.

A view of Dunstable North station taken on 11 July 1953. The two old signals have had the white vertical bands on their red arms painted black. In the background is the bridge carrying the line across the A5 road (Watling Street) to Luton. The use of ordinary chaired track for the turntable circle may be noted, but the healthy weeds suggest that it was seldom used.

Right The tiny station at Stanbridgeford, between Dunstable North and Leighton Buzzard, photographed from my train. It was used in the making of an episode of *The Avengers* TV series just before demolition in October 1968.

Below A driver's-eye view from the footplate of Gresley Class 'N2/2' 0-6-2T No 69554 taken by my father during his goods train trip from Hatfield to Dunstable on Tuesday 26 July 1955. The train is near Wheathampstead. *AD*

The train, at that stage only a brake-van, waits at Harpenden East to let another goods, hauled by a Class 'N7' 0-6-2T, pass. The trimmed laurel and box bushes are a credit to the station staff. *AD*

The smartly dressed guard, holding a shunter's pole for joining and parting the wagons' three-link couplings, poses in front of the engine at Dunstable North station. My father's companion enthusiast is on the footplate. The bracket signals in the background replaced the old signals in my 1953 view on page 106. *AD*

The locomotive taking water from the water crane at the Hatfield end of Luton (Bute Street) station; the driver stands at the wheel of the water valve. The signal, already 'off' for the train, is of the GNR 'somersault' type with its arm pivoted about its centre, designed so that snow on it would not weigh it down to produce a wrong aspect. The signal box is Luton East. *AD*

Minehead

Taunton, in Somerset, was reached by a broad gauge ally of the GWR, the Bristol & Exeter Railway (B&ER) in 1844. The line was initially worked by the GWR, but from 1849 the B&ER started using its own locomotives and rolling-stock. On 31 March 1862 the West Somerset Railway opened a 14-mile branch from Taunton running north-westwards to Watchet on the Bristol Channel. Twelve years later, on 16 July 1874, the Minehead Railway extended the branch 6 miles to reach the town of its name. The branch, as built and as extended, was worked by the B&ER until that company was amalgamated with the GWR in 1876.

From 6 to 13 April 1946 my parents, sister and I visited Minehead to enjoy our first holiday - other than visits to kind members of the family in Derbyshire - since before the Second World War. Film was just becoming available, and fortunately my father took several railway pictures; they are amongst the few pre-nationalisation scenes that I can present.

'Castle', or '4073', Class 4-6-0 No 5003 *Lulworth Castle*, in unlined green livery, at Taunton on Saturday 6 April 1946. The 'Castle' four-cylinder design was by C. B. Collett and dated from 1923, the year of the Grouping. *AD*

Above right In Minehead station in April 1946 stands *Chaffinch*, No 3443 of William Dean's double-framed 4-4-0 'Bulldog' Class, a design originally dating from 1898. *Chaffinch* was one of a 1909 batch, Nos 3441 to 3455, known as the 'Bird' Class, built in Churchward's time. *AD*

Right Collett 0-6-0 goods locomotive No 2211, of the 1930 '2251' Class, takes its dirty train for Taunton out of Minehead in April 1946. The typical GWR lower quadrant signals, signal box and water tower are worth noting. The use of two separate signal brackets at the end of the platform suggests a lack of foresight! *AD*

CHAFFINCH

G W R
BAY

Horsham to Guildford

Although not strictly a branch line - because it linked two main lines instead of being an offshoot from one trunk route - the Horsham to Guildford Direct Railway was just like one. It was authorised by an Act of 6 August 1860, acquired (before completion) by the LB&SCR in 1864, and opened on 2 October 1865. The main lines that it linked belonged to different companies, the LB&SCR and the L&SWR. The former's main line was from London through Three Bridges and Horsham to Ford Junction on the coastal route from Brighton to Portsmouth. Its final stage, from Hardham Junction to Ford Junction, had opened on 3 October 1863. The L&SWR main line was from Waterloo through Woking and Guildford to Portsmouth. This joined the coastal route at Havant, 18 miles west of Ford Junction. The final section, from Godalming to Havant, had opened on 1 January 1859.

The Horsham to Guildford line left the LB&SCR main line 2 miles south-west of Horsham at what was originally called Stammerham Junction. In 1902 the public school Christ's Hospital moved from Newgate Street, in London, to a site to the east of the junction, and a station with platforms on the main line and the Guildford line was opened to serve the school on 28 April of that year. Thereafter the station and junction were called Christ's Hospital; the SR timetable added, in parenthesis, 'West Horsham'. From there the Guildford line ran north-west for 16 miles to Peasmarsh Junction, just over a mile south of Guildford on the L&SWR main line. There was a 381-yard-long tunnel between Rudgwick and Baynards and the boundary between Surrey and Sussex lay across this.

During Southern and early BR days, the trains on the line were hauled mainly by ex-LB&SCR locomotives, including Class 'D1' 0-4-2Ts, 'D3' 0-4-4Ts and 'E4' 0-6-2Ts. Goods trains were worked by 0-6-0s of Classes 'C2', 'C2X' and 'C3'. Former L&SWR Class 'M7' 0-4-4Ts and, in later years, Ivatt LMS-design Class '2' 2-6-2Ts were also used for passenger trains, and Bulleid 'Q1' 0-6-0s for goods.

My father and I visited the line together three times between 1953 and 1965, and I made a return journey along it on 22 May 1965, three weeks before Saturday 12 June, the day of the last ordinary passenger services. We both saw, and photographed, trains at Horsham and Guildford on a number of occasions.

A view of Horsham locomotive depot taken on Saturday 2 March 1963. Ivatt Class '2' 2-6-2T No 41276 was one of the locomotives working the trains to Brighton, via Shoreham, and to Guildford, and will be encountered again in a moment. The Bulleid 'Q1' 0-6-0 is No 33015. The crane in the right background was used for coaling locomotives.

Above Class 'M7' 0-4-4T No 30027, with a train painted in the plain bright red livery of the period, stands at the north end of Horsham station on Saturday 13 May 1950. In the distance are the signal box, opened in April 1938 to replace three boxes dating from 1875, the water tower for the engine shed, and the engine shed itself, a roundhouse.

Below Ivatt LMS-design Class '2' 2-6-2T No 41299 about to leave Christ's Hospital station on a train from Guildford in the afternoon of Saturday 22 May 1965. The junction with the main line is visible in the background. I had just alighted from the train after my return journey to Guildford three weeks before the line closed.

SLINFOLD

Left and above Slinfold was the first station beyond Christ's Hospital, being 2½ miles from there and 4¾ miles from Horsham. A train from Horsham enters the station on Saturday 2 March 1963 (*above*), then pulls away past the signal box (*left*). Although there was no passing loop, there was a small goods yard which may be seen - complete with loading gauge - in the background. The wooden LB&SCR signal post carries an SR metal upper quadrant signal arm. The 6 miles of line from Christ's Hospital to Baynards was a single section worked by 'staff and ticket', and so the signals were not normally used.

Right Ivatt 2-6-2T No 41294 on a train at Rudgwick station, 7 miles from Horsham, on Saturday 3 April 1965. As at Slinfold, there was no passing loop. A signal box, which once controlled a small goods yard at the south end of the platform, is hidden by the train.

Marsh 'C2X' 0-6-0 goods, BR No 32444, a 1910 rebuild of a Billinton Class 'C2' locomotive, stands with a down goods in a siding just north of Baynards station on Saturday 10 October 1953. The picture gives a good view of a loading gauge.

Shortly afterwards a Bulleid Class 'Q1' 0-6-0, No 33003 of the design introduced in 1942 during the Second World War, brings a train of loaded cattle wagons into the station, past the 'C2X' and its train in the siding. Baynards, 8¼ miles from Horsham, and the remaining stations on the journey to Guildford, had up and down platforms so that trains could pass. The shunt signal on the ex-LB&SCR wooden post controlled entry to the siding. *Both AD*

Above A view looking towards Guildford of Cranleigh station, 11¼ miles from Horsham, taken on Saturday 3 April 1963. The signal box on the down platform controlled a goods yard at the Guildford end of the station. One end of an overhead crane is just visible beyond the home signal in the distance. *AD*

Below A down train leaves Bramley & Wonersh station, 16¼ miles from Horsham, on 3 April 1965 behind Ivatt 2-6-2T No 41301; the locomotive is carrying no headcode. The level crossing connected Bramley, to the west, with Wonersh, to the east.

The signalman at Peasmarsh Junction box is about to collect the single-line token from the engine crew of my train from Christ's Hospital on Saturday 22 May 1965. The rails of the Portsmouth main line are visible, as is the junction signal controlling entrance to the Horsham line.

Former LB&SCR 0-6-0 No 32302 of Marsh's 'C3' design, built at Brighton in 1906, stands on a short goods train for the Horsham line in Guildford station on Thursday 15 June 1950. This station was completely rebuilt during the years 1988-9.

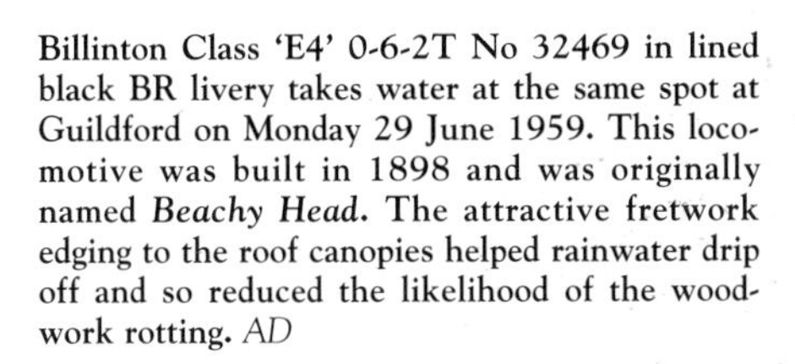

Billinton Class 'E4' 0-6-2T No 32469 in lined black BR livery takes water at the same spot at Guildford on Monday 29 June 1959. This locomotive was built in 1898 and was originally named *Beachy Head*. The attractive fretwork edging to the roof canopies helped rainwater drip off and so reduced the likelihood of the woodwork rotting. *AD*

Ivatt 2-6-2T No 41287 leaves Guildford on a passenger train for Horsham on Saturday 4 May 1963. Note that the fretwork of the platform canopies has been cut away. Guildford is the county town of Surrey and its cathedral is on the skyline at the left of the picture. The slopes of the hill on which the cathedral stands now carry buildings of the university.

Bluebell Railway

The Lewes & East Grinstead Railway was incorporated in 1877 and amalgamated with the LB&SCR in June 1878. It opened on 1 August 1882, running from a new station at East Grinstead 17 miles south to Culver Junction, 3¼ miles out of Lewes on the line to Groombridge. On 3 September 1883 a double-track branch, 4¾ miles long, was opened from Haywards Heath, on the London-Brighton main line, to Horsted Keynes, 6¼ miles down the line from East Grinstead.

To start with, passengers from East Grinstead to London had to travel via Three Bridges on the Brighton main line, but on 10 March 1884 a direct route to London was provided by the opening of a line from East Grinstead through Oxted to South Croydon.

When the Lewes-East Grinstead line was threatened with closure in the mid-1950s, a newspaper campaign was waged in an effort to prevent this. A reporter coined the name 'Bluebell Line', which has been used ever since.

The campaign failed and the last trains ran on 28 May 1955. However, a procedural irregularity was unearthed and the service had to be restored on 7 August 1956. The next attempt at closure was successful and the last BR trains ran on 16 March 1958.

Encouraged by successes in the preservation of Welsh narrow-gauge lines, a society was formed in 1959 (now called the Bluebell Railway Preservation Society) to attempt the reopening of the line. The Society achieved its goal and trains first ran between a temporary station, just south of Horsted Keynes station, and Sheffield Park on 7 August 1960. In April 1985 the Society obtained a Light Railway Order for rebuilding the northern section of the line, and in 1995 trains were running as far as Kingscote, only 2 miles south of East Grinstead.

My father and I travelled the whole length of the Bluebell line from East Grinstead to Lewes and back on 7 May 1955, three weeks before the original closure. He repeated the journey on 4 March 1958, less than a fortnight before the final closure.

On Sunday 1 April 1962, my father and I enjoyed a steam-hauled journey from London Bridge to Sheffield Park and back on the 'Blue Belle', the third of three excursions sponsored by the Bluebell Railway Preservation Society. The train locomotive was Captain W. G. Smith's ex-Great Northern Railway 0-6-0ST No 1247 built in 1902, the subject of Silver Link's *1247:*

BR Standard Class '4' 2-6-4T No 80011 on a train lighter than itself at East Grinstead Low Level station on Wednesday 13 March 1957. The carriages of a train in the High Level station are visible on the bridge. *AD*

Above Captain Smith's ex-GNR 0-6-0ST No 1247, LNER Class 'J52', at Horsted Keynes ready for the return journey of the 'Blue Belle' to London Bridge on Sunday 1 April 1962. Note the conductor rail of the near track. The line through Ardingly to Haywards Heath was not closed until 28 October 1963. *AD*

Preservation Pioneer, written by Capt Smith. On the uphill return from Sheffield Park to Horsted Keynes the Bluebell Railway's Adams '0415' Class 4-4-2T No 488 was at the front of the train, No 1247 at the rear. The timetable for the journey was as follows:

London Bridge	d 10.02 am
Haywards Heath	a 12.00 noon
	d 12.17 pm
Horsted Keynes	a 12.30 pm
	d 12.40 pm
Sheffield Park	a 1.05 pm
Sheffield Park	d 3.35 pm
Horsted Keynes	a 3.50 pm
	d 4.26 pm
Haywards Heath	a 4.40 pm
	d 4.54 pm
London Bridge	a 7.00 pm

The famous Dr Beeching, and his wife, travelled on the train, and a stop was made at 12.45 pm so that he could open a station at Holywell (Waterworks), between Horsted Keynes and Sheffield Park - quite a change for him!

Above right Standard 2-6-4T No 80033, with an extraordinary three-disc headcode, backs on to our train for Lewes on Saturday 7 May 1955 in East Grinstead Low Level station. Note the 'birdcage' lookout of the ex-SE&CR guards van.

Right The fireman puts water into the tanks of No 80033 at the south end of Sheffield Park station on 7 May 1955. The yard to the left of the picture now accommodates the workshop and locomotive shed of the Bluebell Railway Preservation Society.

80033
622

80033

The 12.28 pm train from East Grinstead enters Lewes on 4 March 1958. Class 'E4' 0-6-0T No 32467 has had no weight problem during its journey! The fine display of signals is noteworthy. The lines curving to the right past the signal box are to Hastings. *AD*

Kent & East Sussex Railway

In the 1840s the South Eastern Railway opened its main line from Redhill to Folkestone and Dover. The line ran practically due east through Tonbridge (19½ miles from Redhill, reached on 26 May 1842) and Ashford (26½ miles beyond Tonbridge, reached on 1 December 1842). About ten years later lines were opened from both Tonbridge and Ashford to Hastings. That from Tonbridge - opened on 1 February 1852 - ran south-east through Robertsbridge for 33 miles; the line from Ashford - opened on 13 February 1851 - ran for 26 miles south-west. These three lines enclosed a large triangle of Kent, within which the first place to be served by a railway was Hawkhurst. A branch line to there from Paddock Wood, 5 miles east of Tonbridge, was opened on 4 September 1893. Tenterden, 7 miles east of Hawkhurst and arguably the most important town in the area, did not benefit from this. Various schemes for lines through, or to, Tenterden were put forward. The one actually built ran from Robertsbridge, on the Tonbridge-Hastings line, and eventually reached Headcorn, 16 miles east of Tonbridge.

Originally the powers for building the line were obtained - as required by the Regulation of Railways Act, 1896 - by an Act of Parliament: the Rother Valley (Light) Railway Act of 2 July 1896. Only weeks later, on 14 August, the Light Railways Act was passed under which a light railway could be built, under powers given by a Light Railway Order obtained from the Board of Trade, to standards less stringent, and so less expensive, than those required for a normal railway.

In 1899 Holman Frederick Stephens was appointed General Manager of the Rother Valley Railway (RVR). He recognised the financial advantages of building the line as a light railway under the provisions of the Light Railways Act and obtained a Light Railway Order on 8 December 1899. The line was opened (for passengers) to Tenterden on 2 April 1900 and extended for a mile and a half to a station nearer the town on 15 April 1903. The new terminus was called Tenterden Town and the old, which had become a through station, was renamed Rolvenden. On 1 June 1904 the line was given a grander name, the Kent & East Sussex Railway (K&ESR), and on 15 May the following year it was completed by the opening of an 8-mile extension to Headcorn, halfway between Paddock Wood and Ashford.

During the First World War, Mr Stephens served in the Royal Engineers and achieved the rank of Lieutenant Colonel; it is as Colonel Stephens - the engineer and manager concerned with so many light railways - that he is now remembered. At the time of the 1923 Grouping, his lines could have been merged with the appropriate 'Big Four' companies, but he decided to keep them inde-

At Headcorn on 3 December 1953 are Class 'O1' 0-6-0 goods No 31065, a Wainwright 1908 rebuild of a Stirling Class 'O' engine dating from 1908, and Stroudley/Marsh 'Terrier' Class 'A1X' No 32678. Both of these locomotives have been preserved. The footbridge in the background spans the Tonbridge-Ashford main line. *AD*

Above A request stop signal at High Halden Road photographed from the train on which the ICRS party travelled to Rolvenden on Friday 22 April 1949. The wooden grids at each side of the road were to prevent cattle from straying on to the line.

pendent. He died in 1931, so did not have to consider once more the independence of his railways when nationalisation was effected in 1948.

I visited the K&ESR twice before its closure and partial reopening as a preserved line. My first visit was in a party of Imperial College Railway Society members. We travelled from Headcorn to Rolvenden and back on Friday 22 April 1949. My other visit was on Saturday 18 April 1953 when my father and I went from Waterloo (Eastern) to Bodiam and back via Robertsbridge, in order to see, and photograph, both the railway and the beautiful castle. My father visited the line alone on three other occasions, in May 1951, March 1952 and December 1953, his last visit being only a month before the withdrawal of passenger services on 4 January 1954.

The section of line from Robertsbridge to Tenterden was kept open for freight trains and occasional hop-pickers' specials until 12 June 1961 when, partly as a result of flood damage in 1960, it was finally closed. Fortunately, a preservation society was formed in 1973 which succeeded in reopening the line from Tenterden to Rolvenden in 1974, and plans to reopen it all the way to Robertsbridge.

In its early years the K&ESR had owned locomotives from various sources, not all of them pre-Grouping or 'Big Four' companies. Later on it relied progressively more on locomotives loaned by the Southern Railway and its successor, the Southern Region of British Railways. Stroudley 'Terrier' No 3 was the only K&ESR locomotive I saw during my 1949 visit.

Below 'Terrier' No 32644 brings its train from Rolvenden into Tenterden Town on 22 April 1949 past the extraordinary three-armed signal. This locomotive was built as No 44 *Fulham* in 1877 and was given its new boiler, to convert it from Class 'A1' to Class 'A1X', in 1912. Unfortunately it was not preserved.

Above K&ESR No 3 was built at Brighton as No 70 *Poplar* in 1872. In 1901 it was bought by the Rother Valley Railway and became No 3 *Bodiam*. It is shown at Rolvenden shed after several rebuilds, and the loss of its name, during the ICRS visit. After nationalisation it became BR No 32670 and was used on the last day of passenger services on the line. Happily, it has been preserved on the rejuvenated K&ESR.

Below Class 'O1' 0-6-0 No 1390, still in SR livery, at Rolvenden shed on the same day. This locomotive was on loan from BR Southern Region, and had just hauled the train in which the ICRS party had travelled from Headcorn.

Above Exchanging single-line tokens at Northiam station on 18 April 1953. The locomotive on the train for Robertsbridge is 'Terrier' No 32659, originally LB&SCR No 59 *Cheam* built in 1875 and reboilered in 1922; it did not have the good fortune to be preserved. *AD*

Below Bodiam station photographed on 18 April 1953, the day when my father and I visited the castle. The worked pair of half-points to prevent unauthorised movement into the platform line is interesting, as are the poles and wires supporting the hop plants in the fields behind the station. *AD*

Right 'Terrier' No 32659 about to leave Bodiam station on the same day after our arrival from Robertsbridge. The cattle grids at the level crossing are clearly shown.

S 6638 S
WHIS

ROBERTSBRIDGE
32659

ROBERTSBRIDGE
ROBERTSBRIDGE

Left No 32659 stands in the bay platform at Robertsbridge on a mixed train on 23 March 1951. The name on the private owner wagon behind the coach is AIREDALE. The man in the distance, above the engine, seems to be digging an allotment. *AD*

Below left Our train for Bodiam in Robertsbridge on 18 April 1953. The large station sign reads ROBERTSBRIDGE CHANGE FOR KENT & EAST SUSSEX LINE. The man near the footbridge is my father and a 'Q1' 0-6-0 is visible in the distance. The light patches between the doors to the 1st Class compartments are due to the peeling of the paint.

Hayling Island

Hayling Island, a seaside resort with good beaches, lies just off the South Coast, south of Havant and a few miles east of Portsmouth. The LB&SCR completed its coastal line from Brighton through Havant to Portsmouth in 1847. On 1 January 1859 the L&SWR opened its line from Godalming to Havant, and from the 24th of that month ran trains from London through to Portsmouth. The inhabitants of Hayling Island wished to benefit from the improved rail communication at Havant, and formed a company, which was incorporated as the Hayling Railway Company by an Act of 1860, to build a line from Havant to South Hayling. After several changes of plan, and further Acts of Parliament, the line was finally opened on 8 July 1867.

The particular interest of the Hayling Island branch stemmed from the 1,000-foot-long timber bridge that carried the line from Langstone, on the mainland, to the island. This resulted in the branch being worked for almost all of its existence by the smallest LB&SCR locomotives, the Stroudley 'A1' 'Terriers', which weighed only 27½ tons (and only three-quarters of a ton more after rebuilding as Class 'A1X' by Marsh).

I visited the branch once, on 25 March 1950, with the Imperial College Railway Society while returning from a visit to the Isle of Wight railway system. My father made three visits - in 1955, 1957 and 1959. The line closed on 4 November 1963.

A view from the carriage window as 'Terrier' No 32650 takes the 1.35 pm train away from Havant on 11 October 1955. It was built at Brighton in 1876 as No 50 *Whitechapel* and was reboilered in 1920, becoming No 650 of Class 'A1X'. From 1930 to 1936 the engine was used on the Isle of Wight as No W9 *Fishbourne*, and it later became No 515S, a departmental shunter at Lancing Carriage Works. It is now preserved in the guise of LB&SCR *Sutton* on the Kent & East Sussex Steam Railway. *AD*

BRITISH RAILWAYS

Left 'Terrier' No 32646 had just returned from the Isle of Wight when I travelled behind it from Havant to Hayling Island and back on 25 March 1950. The engine began life in 1876 as LB&SCR No 46 *Newington* and became in turn L&SWR No 734; Freshwater, Yarmouth & Newport Railway No 2; SR No W2 *Freshwater*; SR No 8, still named *Freshwater*; and finally BR No 32646, as illustrated. It is now preserved on the Isle of Wight Steam Railway as W8 *Freshwater*.

Below left 'Terrier' No 32650 on the Havant train in the station on 11 October 1955. The LB&SCR signals retain their original wooden arms. *AD*

Right The train approaches the timber Langston bridge on its way to Havant on 11 October 1955. The cabin part way along the bridge contained the controls for the opening span and the signals on either side. The milepost indicates 1¾ miles from Havant. *AD*

Isle of Wight

The railways on the Isle of Wight had a complicated history. In the following account, the companies that actually built lines are considered chronologically in the order in which the first parts of their lines were opened.

The Cowes & Newport Railway (C&NR) opened its 4¼-mile line between the towns of its title on 1 July 1862. Just over two years later, on 23 August 1864, the Isle of Wight Railway (IWR) opened the first part of its route down the east coast of the island from Ryde to Shanklin (7¼ miles). It completed the route with 4 miles of line from Shanklin to Ventnor, opened on 15 September 1866.

The first attempt at linking the C&NR with the IWR was begun by the Isle of Wight (Newport Junction) Railway (IW(NJ)R), which opened a line from Sandown, on the IWR Ryde to Ventnor line, to Shide, a mile south of Newport, a distance of 8¼ miles. This opening was on 1 February 1875, but it was more than three years later, on 1 June 1879, that the mile of track bringing the line to Newport station was completed. By then another company had linked the C&NR with the IWR.

The Ryde & Newport Railway (R&NR) opened a line from Smallbrook Junction (three-quarters of a mile south of Ryde) to Newport - a distance of 8 miles - on 20 December 1875. The company agreed from the outset to work in conjunction with the C&NR, and the two companies set up a joint committee. In 1880 this committee was instructed by the Official Receiver to operate the IW(NJ)R, bankrupted by the cost of its mile of line from Shide to Newport, which had included a large brick viaduct over the River Medina.

The next extension of the island's railway system was brought about by the joint action of two mainland railway companies, the LB&SCR and the L&SWR, both eager to stimulate traffic on their routes to Portsmouth. These companies extended the line from the then Ryde terminus, which became the St John's Road station, through a station on the Esplanade to a terminus at the end of a new pier. The three-quarter-mile line to Ryde Esplanade was opened on 5 April 1880 and the half-mile continuation to Ryde Pier Head was opened on 12 July of the same year.

On 27 May 1882 a 2¾-mile branch line was opened by the Brading Harbour Railway (BHR) from Brading, on the Ryde to Ventnor line of the IWR, to Bembridge. The branch was worked by the IWR and served a quay from which, until 1888, a ferry was operated to Langston Harbour on the LB&SCR Hayling Island branch. It was absorbed by the IWR in 1898.

The complexity of ownership of the Isle of Wight railways was reduced somewhat on 19 July 1887 when the Ryde & Newport, Cowes & Newport and Isle of Wight (Newport Junction) Railways amalgamated to form the Isle of Wight Central Railway (IWCR). This did not mark the end of railway development, however, because two further companies were to build lines. The first of these was the Freshwater, Yarmouth & Newport Railway (FY&NR), which opened its 12-mile route for goods traffic on 10 September 1888, and for passengers on 20 July 1889. The junction with the C&NR faced Cowes, so trains from Freshwater had to reverse to reach Newport station.

The last company to build a new line was the Newport, Godshill & St Lawrence Railway (NG&StLR). It opened 5½ miles of line from Merstone, on the IWCR Newport to Sandown route, to St Lawrence on 26 July

1897. Just under three years later, on 1 June 1900, it opened a 1¼-mile extension from St Lawrence to a new terminus at Ventnor, bringing the island's route mileage to its maximum of 55½. The terminus was originally called Ventnor Town but was renamed by the SR Ventnor West. The NG& StLR was worked by the IWCR and was amalgamated with it in 1913.

At one time or another, six of the island railway companies just described had locomotives and rolling-stock of their own. After the 1923 Grouping, the SR soon disposed of the miscellaneous locomotives that it inherited and standardised on three Classes: the former LB&SCR 'Terrier' and 'E1' 0-6-0Ts, and the former L&SWR Class 'O2' 0-4-4T. Until 1932 the engine numbers included the prefix 'W'.

My father and I visited the Isle of Wight railways together on four occasions and each of us made two independent visits. On 17 April 1949, with my mother and sister, we travelled from Bournemouth to Freshwater and back on the paddle-steamer *Bournemouth Queen*, and saw a Freshwater train hauled by 'O2' No 25 *Godshill* in SR malachite green livery.

My next visit was with members of the Imperial College Railway Society on 24 and 25 March 1950. We managed to travel over the whole system, spending the night at Ryde. Three of the lines we saw were closed quite soon afterwards: Merstone to Ventnor West on 15 September 1952; and Brading to Bembridge and Newport to Freshwater on 21 September 1953.

My father's and my remaining visits to the Isle of Wight were all made via the Mid-Sussex line and the ferry from Portsmouth Harbour to Ryde. In those days there was an electric train service from Victoria through Epsom, Dorking and Horsham to Portsmouth. The trains did not stop at Epsom, but we joined (and left) them at Dorking. Our visits spanned the period from 1955 to 1966, the last on Saturday 19 February 1966 being made two days before closure of the Smallbrook Junction to Cowes line. Saturday 31 December 1966 saw the last BR steam service, from Ryde to Shanklin, run. The section of the line from Shanklin to Ventnor had been closed on 18 April of that year. On 20 March 1967 BR introduced an electric train service from Ryde to Shanklin using refurbished pre-1938 London 'tube' stock. Between 1989 and 1990 this stock was replaced by refurbished 1938 stock, designated Class 483.

Happily, it is still possible to enjoy a steam train journey on the island because the Isle of Wight Steam Railway has preserved the 5-mile portion of the Ryde-Newport line from Wootton through Haven Street to Smallbrook Junction, and a station has been built there allowing interchange between the Society's trains and the BR electric services.

Locomotive No 32 *Bonchurch* about to leave Freshwater on the first stage of the Imperial College Railway Society (ICRS) tour of the island on 24 March 1950. It is in the beautiful lined malachite green livery of the period. The work done to lengthen and heighten the platform is clearly shown.

Above Members of the ICRS party at Newport shed on the same day. The locomotive at the hoist is Stroudley Class 'E1' No 3 *Ryde*, built in 1881 as LB&SCR No 154 *Madrid*, which was scrapped in 1959. On this side of the hoist are two pairs of wheels from a ganger's trolley. The engine at the left is No 29 *Alverstone*, and No 35 *Freshwater* is just inside the shed.

Below A later view of engines at Newport shed, taken on Monday 19 September 1955. From left to right they are Nos 33 *Bembridge* and 29 *Alverstone* again, originally numbered 218 and 202, both of Class 'O2', and No 4 *Wroxall*, an ex-LB&SCR 0-6-0T of Stroudley's 'E1' Class, built as No 131 *Gournay* in 1878. No 4 was scrapped in 1960. *AD*

Above When I took this picture at Sandown I was waiting with other members of the ICRS party for our train to Newport. Class 'O2' tank No 18 *Ningwood* is on a train for Ventnor at about 6.00 pm on 24 March 1950. Note the painted metal destination board on the side of the first carriage between the windows of the guard's compartment and the first passenger compartment.

Below Another scene at Sandown showing the signal box that sprouted out of the station canopy. My father took this picture on Monday 16 January 1956. The locomotive, No 24 *Calbourne*, is the 'O2' tank now preserved. The smokebox door carries an elliptical plate giving the shed code '70H' for Ryde. *AD*

No 14 *Fishbourne* waits to take the 11.32 am train from Bembridge to Brading on the second day of the ICRS tour of the island's railways, Saturday 25 March 1950. A small turntable at the end of the platform was used to release the engine of an incoming train, a feature probably unique at this date but quite common in the early days of railways. The cleanliness of the locomotive and train is to be admired - most trains on the mainland were not so well kept.

No 19 *Osborne* at Ventnor station on 25 March 1950, resplendent in Southern malachite green livery. In the background is the entrance to the St Boniface Down Tunnel, 1,312 yards long. Ventnor station is 276 feet above sea level. It has always seemed strange to the author that when the eastern route down the island was electrified, the section from Shanklin to Ventnor was not included; the tube stock used would have felt at home in the tunnel!

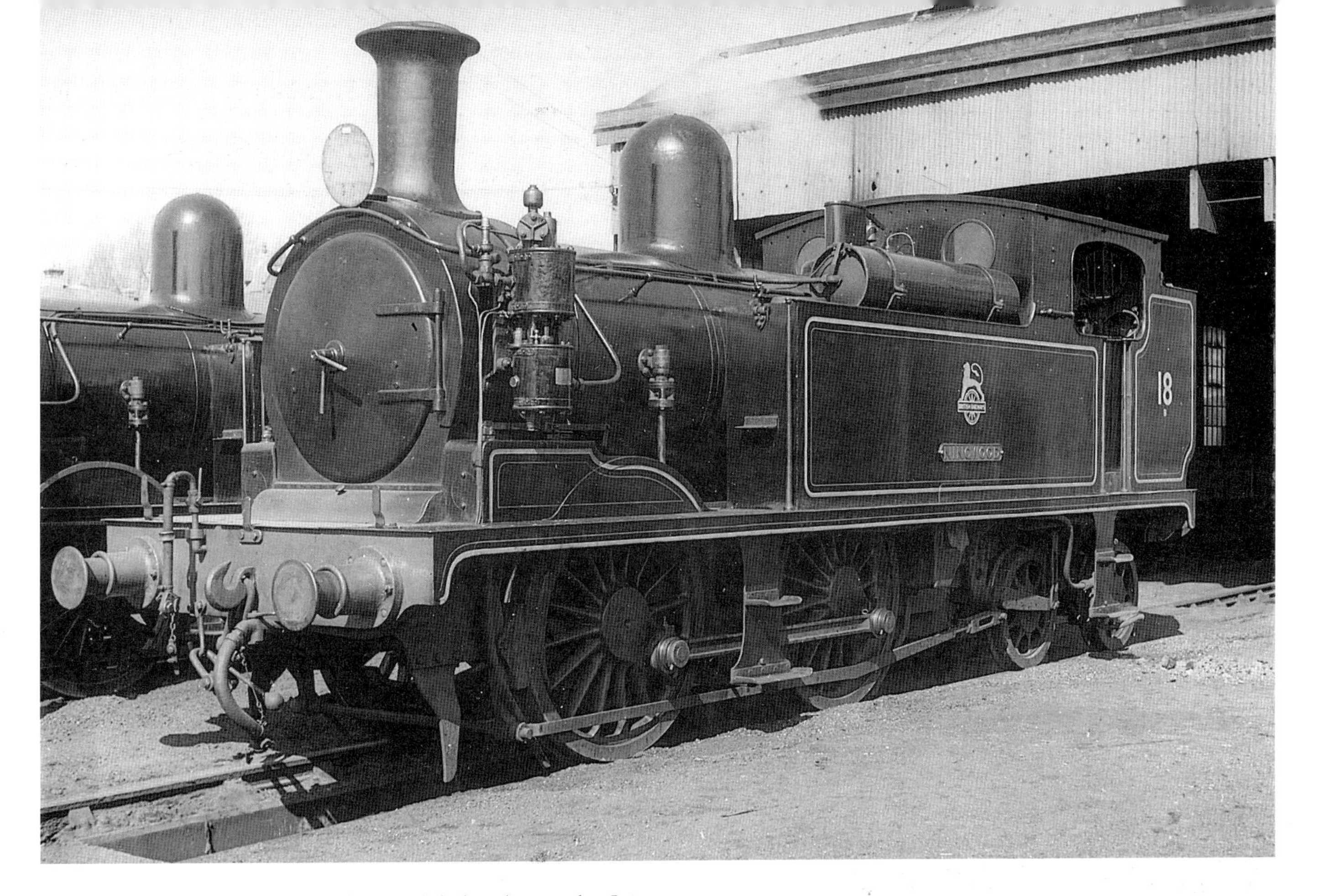

Above No 18 *Ningwood* at Ryde St John's Road shed on the same day. It is interesting to note that the lining goes near the top of the coal bunker, whereas on some locomotives (for example Nos 14 and 21) it remained in line with that near the top of the water tank. The cylinder on the tank was a compressed air supply for the brakes.

Below A malachite green 'O2', No 15 *Cowes*, takes a train from Cowes on the double-track section from Ryde St John's Road to Ryde Pier Head during the ICRS tour. The tall signal post was to render the upper arm visible above the bridge at the north end of the station.

Left An engineman fiddles with the Westinghouse brake pump of No 21 *Sandown* at Ryde Esplanade station on 25 March 1950. In the background two cars of the Ryde Pier Tramway, which ran to the end of the old pier, may be seen. This tramway opened, with horse traction, on 29 August 1864, and between the years 1871 and 1880 ran to the original terminus of the IWR. When the railway was extended to Ryde Pier Head using part of the tramway route, the tramway was once again restricted to operation along the pier. As well as horse traction, steam, electric, petrol and diesel power were all used. The tramway was closed on 26 January 1969.

Below A train leaves Ryde Pier Head station behind 'O2' No 14 *Fishbourne* on Wednesday 2 October 1957; the tracks of the Ryde Pier Tramway are in the foreground. The South Coast is visible on the horizon. *AD*

Right Class 'O2' locomotive No 24 *Calbourne* (now preserved) stands partly dismantled at the St John's Road Works on 25 March 1950, the second day of the ICRS visit to the island. It is interesting to see how the driving wheels came above the running plate; the inner portions of the water tanks would have constituted their splashers. The heavy reduction gearing suggests that the locomotive hoist was man-powered.

3
4
24

A scene at Cowes on the last Saturday of operation of the Ryde to Cowes service, 21 February 1966.
The locomotive is No 24 *Calbourne* again, completed as L&SWR No 209 at Nine Elms in December 1891, and now preserved by the Isle of Wight Steam Railway.

4. Shed visits

A visit to an engine shed was one of the great pleasures of a railway enthusiast's life during the steam era. British Railways kindly gave shed permits to groups or individuals promptly and without demur. One could not always predict when one would be near to a shed, but a visit to the office of the shed foreman would nearly always result in his giving one permission to look round. Locomotive men were kindly folk, sympathetic towards the genuine enthusiast; many had started their careers with the pre-Grouping companies.

Some sheds, such as Feltham, Ryde St John's Road and Whitby, could be seen and photographed well from nearby. Nevertheless a permit was still desirable, allowing more varied and better-placed pictures to be taken. Between 1945 and the end of steam in the South of England, in April 1967, I visited about 50 sheds, some of them more than once, taking photographs at all of them.

The particular pleasures of a shed visit were many. One could see the interesting locomotives tucked away inside, including those being worked on; not all repairs had to be carried out at a main workshop. One could see the oiling, watering and coaling, and the clearing of ash out of the firebox and smokebox, necessary for keeping an engine in running order. At the bigger sheds the coaling plants were of interest in themselves. In some, loaded coal wagons were lifted bodily and tipped to empty their contents into a locomotive tender or bunker. One had to watch one's step to avoid treading on red-hot ash, falling into an inspection pit, or being run over by a locomotive. All pervading were the smoke and smell from burning coal, fragrant to the enthusiast if upsetting for today's environmentalist!

Dalry Road

Dalry Road shed lay between Dalry Road station on the lines to Granton and Leith and the line running south-west to Carstairs. It supplied locomotives for passenger services from Edinburgh, Princes Street - just over a mile to the east - to Carlisle, Carstairs, Glasgow and Perth, and also for local goods and passenger trains. It was built for the Caledonian Railway (CR) and passed to the LMS at the 1923 Grouping. After nationalisation it survived until October 1965.

My father and I visited Dalry Road, armed with the necessary permit, on Wednesday 12 July 1950 during the family holiday referred to in the Edinburgh section of this book.

The coaling stage of the shed as seen from Dalry Road station. The ex-CR 0-6-0 that has pushed loaded wagons into the shed covering the coaling stage is No 57645, shown in detail on page 146. The two 4-6-0s are of the 'Jubilee' Class. *AD*

Above A general view of the depot, the largest of the three sheds being in the centre. The identifiable locomotives are No 55139, on the left, a McIntosh '92' Class (LMS Class '2P') 0-4-4T built at St Rollox in 1899 as No 881, and, by the water-crane, LMS Fairburn 1945-design Class '4P' 2-6-4T No 42269.

Below One of only four 'Black Staniers' to be named in LMS days - No 45156 *Ayrshire Yeomanry*. Curiously, D. S. Barrie's *Modern Locomotives of the LMS* and the 1943 Ian Allan *ABC* give a fifth name, *Queen's Edinburgh*, for No 5155, which is not given in later works. Perhaps the name was never carried. Note the single-line token exchange mechanism on the cab side. The somewhat leaky roof of Dalry Road station awning is in the background.

McIntosh CR '439' Class 0-4-4T (LMS Class '2P'), built at St Rollox in 1900 as No 446, is seen (*above*) in early BR livery as No 55166. The second photograph shows 0-4-4T No 55165. Comparison between the two shows how the appearance of a locomotive can be marred by an ugly chimney; also, how important is the style of lettering. The Class '5' 4-6-0 behind No 55165, No 44793, has - most unusually for a former LMS locomotive - the name of its shed (Polmadie) painted on the buffer beam in addition to the customary elliptical plate.

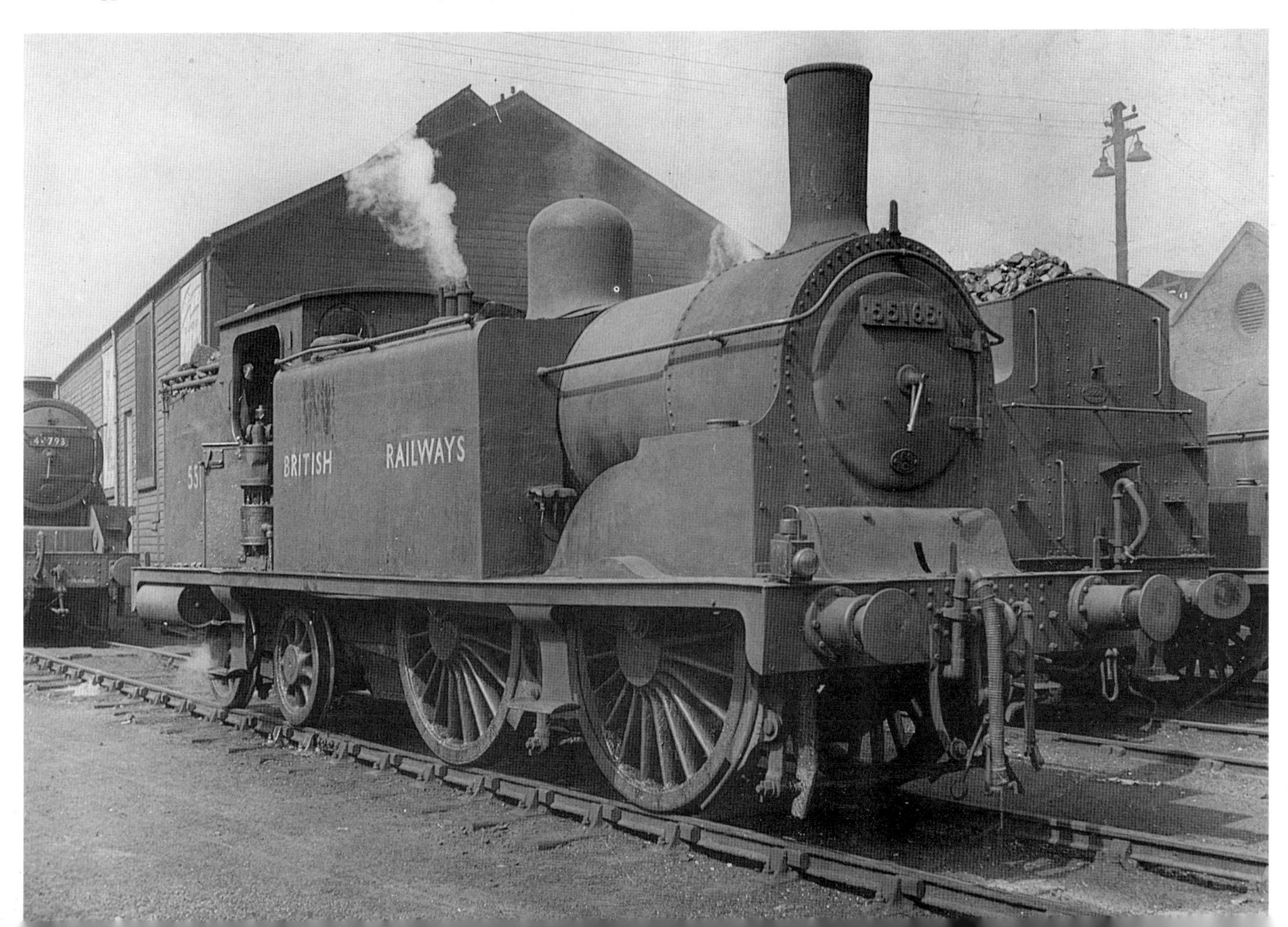

Above Pickersgill's 1916 design of CR 4-4-0, originally No 73, as British Railways No 54478 at Dalry Road. Forty-eight of these locomotives were built and all were taken into BR stock. They were withdrawn between 1953 and 1963.

Below The highest numbered - under the LMS and BR - member of McIntosh's '652' Class, 0-6-0 No 57645. It was built as No 460 in 1909 and renumbered 661 in 1918. There were 17 locomotives of this Class. Note the shovels and pokers disposed around the ash-pit to trip the unwary. CR No 828 (later LMS Class '3F' No 17566) of the very similar '812' Class is preserved on the Strathspey Railway; it was built at St Rollox Works in 1899.

Haymarket

Haymarket shed, about a mile and a half west of Edinburgh's Waverley station, was the principal NBR shed in the city. It was rebuilt in 1894 following the opening of the Forth Bridge. My father and I visited it on Tuesday 11 July 1950, during our second Edinburgh holiday. Although Haymarket cared for express locomotives used on the East Coast Main Line, the pictures I took that day gave no indication of that fact.

Holmes NBR Class 'C' 0-6-0 goods locomotive built in 1891 as No 673. It received its name *Maude* after service overseas during the First World War. It was renumbered by the LNER at the Grouping of 1923 as 9673 (Class 'J36'), and again in the 1946 renumbering as 5243. Finally, British Railways added 60000 at some time after 1 January 1948. This locomotive has been preserved on the Bo'ness & Kinneil Railway.

Sir Nigel Gresley had 24 further locomotives of Robinson's GCR 'Director' Class 4-4-0 (LNER Class 'D11') built by Kitson's in 1924 for use in Scotland. *Luckie Mucklebackit*, named - like the remainder - after a character in one of Sir Walter Scott's novels, was No 6385 before the 1946 renumbering. One of the 11 original GCR locomotives, No 506 *Butler-Henderson* (BR No 62660) has been preserved.

One of Gresley's small-wheeled (4 ft 8 in) 0-6-0 goods engines, Class 'J38' No 65924 from Dunfermline shed. The letters LNER are clearly visible on the tender. Only 35 of this Class, introduced in 1926, were built, whereas 271 of the 5 ft 2 in wheeled 0-6-0s of Class 'J39' were constructed between 1926 and 1941. The eccentric on the centre wheel driving the mechanical lubricator on the running plate is worth noting.

In well-cleaned LNER livery is former NBR Holmes Class 'F' 0-6-0T No 844, first LNER No 9844 and post-1946 No 8328. This attractive design was intended purely for shunting, having neither spring buffers nor vacuum brake.

St Margaret's

St Margaret's was the former NBR shed to the east of Edinburgh Waverley station and supplied locomotives for local passenger and goods services. It did not have to house the whole of its allocation, there being a number of sub-sheds in the district where engines could spend hours out of use. The shed closed in April 1967.

My father and I visited St Margaret's twice, in 1948 and 1950.

Below On my first view of St Margaret's shed, on Wednesday 18 August 1948, I was excited to find the last two ex-GER 2-4-2Ts of Class 'F7', nicknamed 'Crystal Palaces' because of their large window-cabs. Nos 7093 and 7094, shown here, were in a siding east of the shed with 'J69' 0-6-0T No 8562, seen to the left, and 'Y9' No 68111. Twelve 'F7' tanks were built in 1909 to J. Holden's design and were GER Nos 1300 to 1311, LNER 8300 to 8311. In 1942 six survivors were renumbered 7593 to 7598, and in 1946 the two of these remaining, Nos 7597 and 7598, were renumbered 7093 and 7094. They were withdrawn in the year that I saw them and would not have had 60000 added to their numbers.

Bottom One of Reid's 1910-design 0-6-2Ts built for the NBR, LNER Class 'N15/1', bearing its BR No in LNER transfers and shunting near the shed on the same day. The NBR built 69 of these locomotives; the LNER 30 more in 1924. The lettering on the wagon behind reads: 'Not to leave St Margarets shed'.

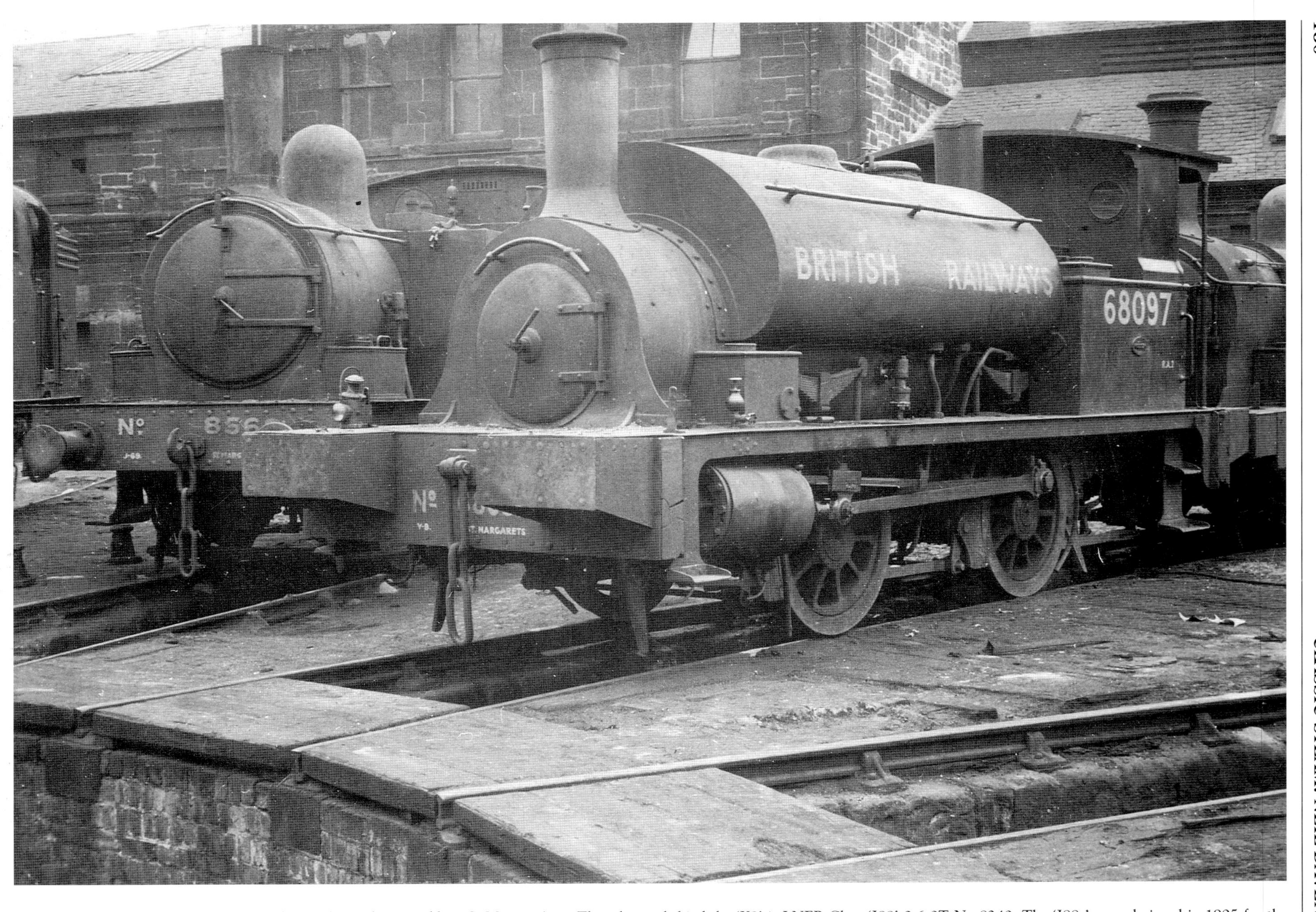

Holmes NBR Class 'G' (LNER Class 'Y9') 0-4-0ST at the turntable at St Margaret's on Thursday 19 August 1948. This locomotive was originally NBR No 1098, then LNER No 10098, and, after 1946, 8097, before receiving the BR number shown. The 'Y9' that became BR No 68095 (NBR 1094) has been preserved. An ex-GER 'J69' 0-6-0T (probably No 8562) is to the left, while behind the 'Y9' is LNER Class 'J88' 0-6-0T No 8340. The 'J88s' were designed in 1905 for the NBR by Reid, and No 8340 was earlier NBR No 116 and LNER 9116. As with the 'Y9s', the 'J88s' had block buffers and no vacuum brake for passenger working.

Above Reid 4-4-2T NBR Class 'L', LNER Class 'C16', No 7497 at the west end of the shed on 19 August 1948. It was, before 1946, No 9511 (NBR No 511) and would later have been renumbered 67497. The 21 locomotives of this Class were withdrawn between 1955 and 1961.

Below Ex-LNER Class 'J36' 0-6-0 as British Railways No 65224 *Mons* inside the shed on Tuesday 11 July 1950. Note the tender cab for more comfortable backward running. Before 1946 this engine was LNER No 9648, the NBR number having been 648. Twenty-four of these locomotives, which served overseas during the First World War, were named, and *Maude*, seen on page 147, has been preserved. Note the locomotive parts - a coupling rod, cylinder cover and piston - on the shed floor.

Also photographed on 11 July 1950 was Fowler '2F' 0-6-0T No 47162, one of ten locomotives built in 1928 with a short wheelbase for shunting in dockyard or other sidings containing sharp curves. This former LMS engine was still allocated to St Margaret's in 1959.

Hellifield

Hellifield once had two locomotive sheds, one opened in 1880 by the Midland Railway (MR) on its Settle-Carlisle line and the other opened in 1881 by the Lancashire & Yorkshire Railway (L&YR) at the end of its line running north-east from Blackburn. The latter shed was closed by the LMS in November 1927, but the former remained open until 17 June 1963, and was subsequently used for storing a number of preserved locomotives. British Railways' last steam passenger train ran past on 11 August 1968.

My father and I visited Hellifield shed on 1 July 1950 during a planned break in our journey to Hawes for the family summer holiday.

A general view of the shed showing, on the left, ex-LMS Class '2P' 2-6-2T No 1205 of Ivatt's 1946 design, Stanier Class '5' 4-6-0 No 44726 and Stanier Class '3P' 2-6-2T No 40183 taking water on the line leading to the turntable. A total of 139 of the '3P' tanks were built from 1935 onwards. *AD*

Above Fowler Compound Class '4P' 4-4-0 No 41087 at the southern side of the shed. It was built at Derby in 1925 and withdrawn towards the end of 1954. The brick chimney behind the engines belonged to a furnace used for drying sand for locomotive sanding gear. It is a pity that the original arms of the MR signal have been replaced with LMS upper quadrant ones. *AD*

Below A picturesque ex-Pullman car body used as a shed near the carriage sidings.

Left Inside the shed was an ex-L&YR 0-6-0 of Aspinall's 1889 design (Class '27', LMS Class '3F'), of which 448 were built; originally No 99, it is shown as BR No 52445. One of this Class, L&YR No 1300, later BR No 52322, has been preserved.

Below An L&YR Horwich-built Aspinall 2-4-2T of 1889 design in the carriage sidings. Originally No 1012, it became LMS No 10625 (Class '2P') and BR No 50625. Another engine of this 309-strong class, L&YR No 1008 (LMS No 10621 and BR No 50621) has been preserved as part of the National Collection.

Neasden

Neasden was the GCR's London shed for locomotives used on passenger trains out of Marylebone and local freight services. It was just south of the junction of the GCR London Extension, opened in 1899, and the connection to Northolt Junction, on the GW&GC Joint line through Princes Risborough, which opened in 1906. When I first visited the shed with a camera, in 1947, Metropolitan Railway steam locomotives transferred to LNER stock in 1937 were still in evidence. Unfortunately a hole in the bellows of the VPK spoiled my picture of 0-6-4T No 9076. The pictures I include here were taken on Wednesday 20 October 1948 during an ICRS visit.

One of 21 inside-cylinder 4-6-2Ts built to Robinson's 1911 design for the GCR (Class '9N', LNER Class 'A5/1'). It is still in LNER livery, but with its number (9808) prefixed with the letter 'E' (for Eastern Region) in accordance with the system used for some months after nationalisation. Twenty-three more locomotives of this class, slightly modified, were built by the LNER between 1925 and 1926. In the background are coach bodies from early Metropolitan electric stock, and the top of the coaling plant.

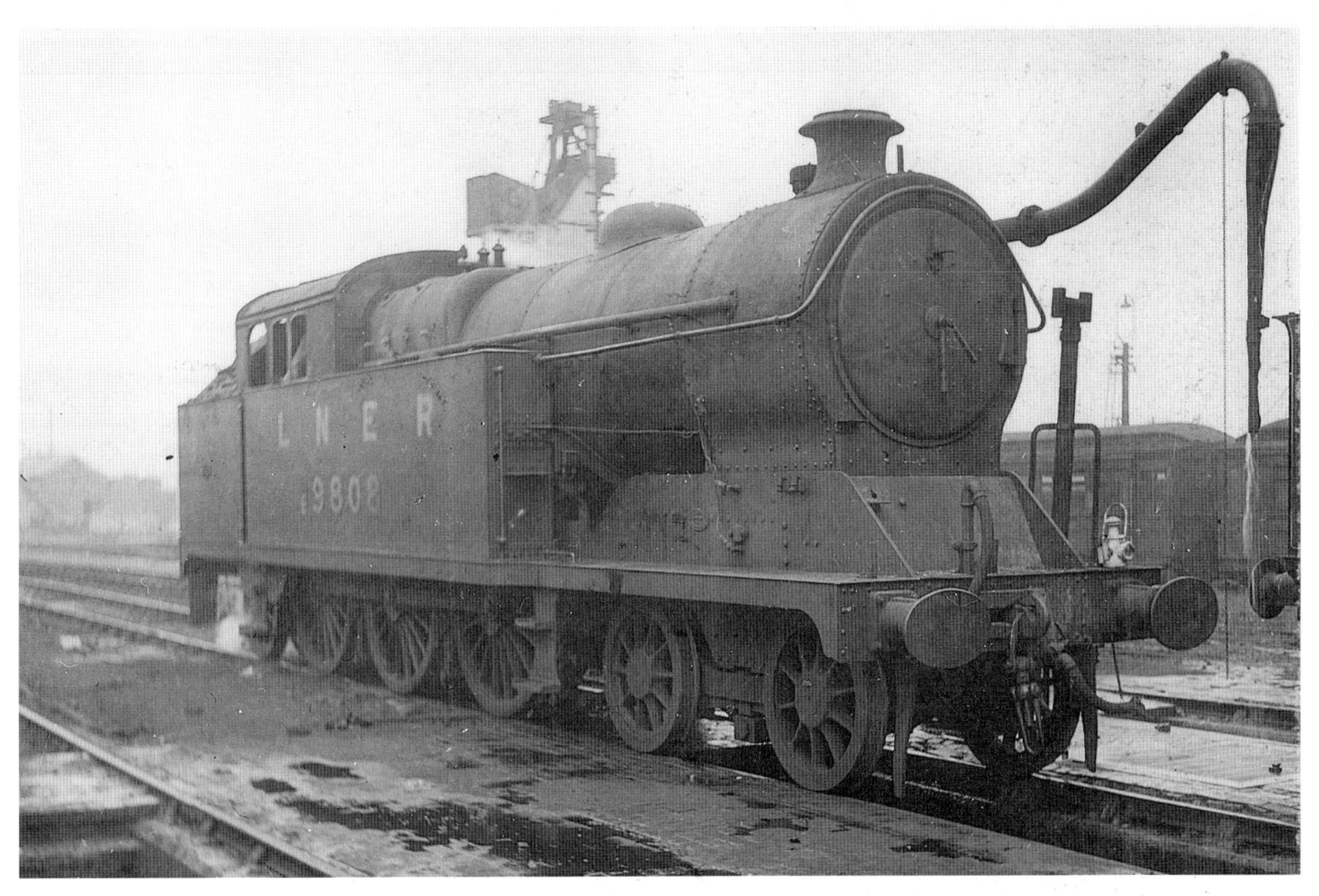

A Robinson inside-cylinder 2-6-4T (GCR class '1B', LNER Class 'L1' until 1945, then Class 'L3'), BR No 69055. This locomotive was GCR No 336 and LNER 5336 before the 1946 renumbering. The LNER class designation was changed to allow 'L1' to be used for Thompson's new 2-6-4T design of 1945. The engines of that class were originally numbered from 9000 up, but were renumbered from 67701 by BR. A War Department 2-8-0 can be glimpsed in the background.

Above The Parker 0-6-2T design of 1891 for the Manchester, Sheffield & Lincolnshire Railway, which became the Great Central Railway in 1897. This example, LNER No 9257 (Class 'N5/2'), was earlier GCR No 523 and LNER No 5523. Leaking steam behind is an 'L3' 2-6-4T.

Below One of the early, named, members of Thompson's 1942 Class 'B1' 4-6-0s, No 1028 *Umseke*, in LNER apple green livery. The number of these locomotives built, 409, seems to have been determined by the numbers available before the first number, 61410, of the 'B16' 4-6-0s!

Camden

Camden, coded 1B, was the London motive power depot that supplied and serviced express passenger locomotives for the trains on the LNWR - subsequently LMS and London Midland Region - main line from Euston to Crewe and thence to North Wales, Liverpool, Manchester and Scotland. It was there that one saw the 'Royal Scot' 4-6-0s and Stanier 'Pacifics' that were the cream of LMS motive power. I visited the shed three times, the two last with the Imperial College Railway Society, but saw locomotives there quite often when travelling to and from Euston.

The 69 members of Fowler's 1927 'Royal Scot' Class were all ultimately rebuilt with a taper boiler and double chimney, but this picture, taken on Tuesday 8 March 1949, the day of the first ICRS visit, shows No 46140 *The King's Royal Rifle Corps* in its original form on the turntable at the western end of Camden shed in well-cleaned early BR lined black livery.

Seen on the same day is rebuilt 'Royal Scot' No 46118 *Royal Welch Fusilier* in the last LMS livery - black with maroon and straw-coloured lining and lettering. These locomotives were later fitted with rather small and ugly smoke deflectors as shown in the picture of No 46138 overleaf.

A view of Camden shed taken on Saturday 30 June 1951 from the 7.31 am train from Harrow & Wealdstone to Euston, a steam service hauled that day by Stanier 2-6-4T No 42589. The identifiable locomotives are Nos 45680 *Camperdown*, a '5XP' 'Jubilee' Class 4-6-0, and 46138 *The London Irish Rifleman*, a '6P' rebuilt 'Royal Scot'. Beyond it is a 'Patriot', or 'Baby Scot', '5XP' 4-6-0. The top of the coaling plant is visible beyond the building with the chimney.

A view of the western end of the shed, also taken from a passing train but in June 1964. 'Black Stanier' No 44831 stands in front of the water tower and scaffolded coaling plant. The fireman is watering the coal in the tender to keep down dust. To the left is English Electric Type 7 1Co-Co1 diesel-electric locomotive No D221 of the design introduced in 1958. Under the 'TOPS' numbering scheme of 1968 it became Class 40 No 40 021.

Below Stanier Class '5XP' 'Jubilee' 4-6-0 No 45638 *Zanzibar* at the eastern end of the shed on 8 March 1949. The locomotive is in the final LMS livery but carries its British Railways number. Some 190 engines of this 1934 three-cylinder design were built. Teething troubles causing poor steaming of the first to be built were overcome, and the 'Jubilees' became fine locomotives. *Bahamas* (No 5596), *Galatea* (5699), *Kolhapur* (5593) and *Leander* (5690) have been preserved.

Bottom Another 'Jubilee' newly painted in British Railways lined black livery, No 45721 *Impregnable*. Note the Fowler design of tender with coal rails to increase the capacity. This photograph was taken in April 1949. *AD*

Right 'Princess Royal' Class 'Pacific' No 46205 *Princess Victoria* on the turntable at the west end of the shed. This locomotive had been fitted, in 1947, with rocking levers enabling the outside Walschaerts valve gear to work the valves of the two inside cylinders. *AD*

Below right Stanier 'Princess Coronation' Class '7P' 'Pacific' No 46246 *City of Manchester* at the London end of the shed on 8 March 1949. This locomotive was originally streamlined, as indicated by the downward slope at the front of the smokebox. Normal smokeboxes were subsequently fitted to all the 'de-streamlined' engines, Nos 46220 to 46229 and 46235 to 46248. The locomotive is in the British Railways style of lining.

46205

CITY OF MANCHESTER
46246
7P

Rebuilt 'Royal Scot' Class '6' 4-6-0 No 6119 *Lancashire Fusilier* at the London end of the shed on 8 March 1949. The unlined black livery with handpainted number shows that wartime austerity had not yet been superseded on all main-line locomotives. The double sand box on the running plate for supplying the clearly visible sand pipes may be noted; sand could be blown between wheel and rail by steam to improve adhesion when the rails were wet or greasy.

Willesden

Willesden shed, coded '1A', the main district depot on the line out of Euston, was to the south of that line just west of Willesden Junction station. I visited it on Wednesday 25 May 1949 with other members of the Imperial College Railway Society.

Willesden supplied locomotives for all but the principal express trains from Euston and in 1950 had an allocation of 135 - predominantly goods and mixed-traffic classes. There were two actual sheds, one a roundhouse and the other a 12-road shed, with three through roads, on the south side. It was closed in 1965.

Ivatt's 2-6-0 tender engine design of 1946, Class '2F', for lighter duties on the LMS; the equivalent Class '2P' 2-6-2T is shown elsewhere in this book. No 46432 stands in front of Fowler Class '3P' 2-6-2T No 50 in the yard at Willesden.

Above A view inside the roundhouse. From left to right are Class '5' 4-6-0s Nos 5025 - 26th of the 1934 design, which, with variants, was to include 842 engines - and 45071, and a 'Baby Scot' Class '5XP' 4-6-0, almost certainly No 5509 (unnamed). The elongated hoods over the locomotive chimneys gave drivers some latitude in parking.

Below Harbingers of doom for the steam locomotive: the two 1,600 hp Co-Co diesel-electric locomotives designed by H. G. Ivatt and the English Electric Company, and built at Derby. No 10000 was completed just before nationalisation (and thus bears the letters LMS), and No 10001 just after. The locomotives were used together on the heaviest expresses from Euston. In 1948 No 10000 had been used alone on St Pancras to Manchester services.

Above An ugly variant of Stanier's Class '5' design, No 44751, one of the 11 locomotives (44747-57) introduced in 1948 having both Caprotti valve gear and roller bearings.

Below Former MR Johnson Class '2F' 0-6-0 goods No 3561. The MR built 935 engines based on this 1875 design, later examples being provided with larger boilers and being classified '3F'. Some smaller-boilered engines were rebuilt with larger boilers; surprisingly, some were later re-equipped with smaller boilers. At the left of the picture is a Fowler 0-6-0T Class '3F' of 1924, No 47399.

Above Hughes-Fowler 2-6-0 No 2747 (before 1934, No 13047), with steam emerging from its cylinder drain cocks, stands in line with ex-LNWR 0-8-0s. Work on this Hughes design was well advanced at the L&YR Horwich Works at the time of the Grouping (1 January 1923), and Fowler made only minor modifications in completing it.

Below Stanier taper-boiler 2-6-0 Class '5P4F' (later '5F') No 42966. This was Stanier's first design, built in 1933, and in it he tried out many of the Churchward (GWR) features that he was planning to use in his further new types of locomotive for the LMS. The 40 locomotives built to this design supplemented the 245 2-6-0s of the Hughes-Fowler 1926 type; their design was, allegedly, a modification of the Hughes-Fowler, but apart from having similar cabs they looked altogether different.

Former MR Johnson '2F' 0-6-0 No 3725. Comparison with No 3561 on page 164 shows a somewhat larger design of cab fitted by Deeley when the locomotive was given a Belpaire, instead of a round-topped, firebox. The mechanised coaling plant is in the background.

Former LNWR 0-8-0 No 49296, still carrying an LNW-design chimney. This locomotive was originally of Bowen-Cooke's 'G1' Class (LMS Class '6F') but was rebuilt as Class 'G2a' (LMS Class '7F'). Note the sand boxes built into the splashers of the leading two pairs of driving wheels.

Devons Road

Devons Road shed, just west of Bromley (by Bow) station on the Fenchurch Street to Southend line, was the principal engine shed of the North London Railway (NLR). It stabled a considerable number of Fowler '3F' 0-6-0Ts for working freight trains to goods depots and docks in East London, and '4P' 2-6-4Ts for suburban services. However, the engines that provided the lure for enthusiasts were those of the NLR and London, Tilbury & Southend Railway (LT&SR). I visited the shed twice: with my fellow enthusiast Derek Lee on Saturday 11 June 1949 and with members of the Imperial College Railway Society on Wednesday 17 May 1950.

A line of former LT&SR 4-4-2Ts photographed at Devon Road on 11 June 1949. The locomotive in front is No 41959. This was originally No 43 *Great Ilford* and became MR No 2152 in 1912, LMS No 2141 Class '3P' in 1930, and BR No 41959 (as shown) in 1948. There were initially 16 locomotives in this Class, built in 1897-8 and rebuilt in 1909, to Whitelegg's design, but a further 35 were built between 1923 and 1930 for the LMS. LT&SR No 80 *Thundersley* (BR No 41966) has been preserved.

A general view of Devons Road shed taken on 11 June 1949; the line of LT&SR 4-4-2Ts shown overleaf is on the left. The nearby locomotive, of Park's 1887 NLR design, is BR No 58853. It had previously carried the numbers 64 (NLR), 2882 (LNWR), 7512 and, after 1934, 27512 (LMS). Two other 0-6-0Ts of this '2F' Class and four Fowler '3F' 0-6-0Ts are in the distance.

Above For years the oldest LMS locomotive was this crane tank. It was built by Sharp Stewart in 1858 as an 0-4-0T and rebuilt as an 0-4-2T with crane in 1872. It carried in succession the numbers 37, 29 and 29A of the NLR, 2896 of the LNWR, 7217 and 27217 of the LMS, and the number shown of British Railways. It was taken to Derby for scrapping in December 1950, only six months after the date of this picture.

Below Former MR Johnson 0-4-4T No 1295, LMS Class '1P'. Of the 205 of these locomotives built - 30 with 5 ft 7 in instead of 5 ft 4 in driving wheels - 62 were taken into BR stock. No 1295 was allocated BR No 58045, but may not have survived to carry it. The last locomotive of the Class was withdrawn in 1960.

Ex-NLR 0-6-0T No 15 (LNWR No 2875) with its final LMS number 27514 and an elegant NLR chimney stands in front of No 58853 fitted with an LNWR chimney, on 11 June 1949. Thirty of these locomotives were built at Bow Works between 1887 and 1905; 14 were taken into BR stock and one, No 58850, has been preserved on the Bluebell Railway.

Feltham

At Feltham, on the line from Waterloo to Staines, the L&SWR built a concentration yard, at which goods trains could be broken up and the wagons marshalled into trains for different destinations by hump shunting; the yard was opened in 1922. A train from one of eight reception sidings was slowly pushed up a 1 in 140 gradient to the top of a hump where a wagon, or group of wagons, for a particular destination was uncoupled and allowed to run down a 1 in 50 gradient into a marshalling siding where a train for that destination was assembled. There were 19 marshalling sidings, the points at the entrances to each being controlled from a point box.

From Feltham yard trains could reach all parts of the L&SWR, the LNWR and NLR lines at Willesden, the GCR and Metropolitan lines at Neasden, the MR at Brent and the LB&SCR and SE&CR at Clapham Junction.

A locomotive shed at the London end of the yard was rebuilt by the SR between the wars. It housed six through roads and was 475 feet long. There was a 65-foot turntable and a coaling plant of 200 tons capacity, both electrically operated.

My father and I often went to look at, and photograph, Feltham shed because wasteland alongside gave a perfect view. On 1 March 1950 I visited the shed and yard with an ICRS party and was able to see its operation in more detail.

One of the four Urie 1921 'G16' Class 4-8-0Ts used for pushing goods trains up the shunting hump at Feltham yard. Its number, S494, includes the 'S' prefix used immediately after nationalisation to designate former SR locomotives. Note the downward slope of the front of the water tank provided to give the driver a better view. These locomotives were withdrawn between 1959 and 1962.

One of the half-dozen satisfactory pictures I took before nationalisation is this view of Class 'T1' 0-4-4T No 9 at Feltham on Monday 10 November 1947. This locomotive of Adams design was built for the L&SWR in August 1894 and withdrawn in 1948. Initially it was designated Class 'F6', a variant of the original 'T1' design of 1888.

Adams '0395' Class 0-6-0 at the side of the shed on Saturday 31 December 1949. It was built for the L&SWR in 1883 by Neilson & Co of Glasgow. Originally No 433, it became No 0433 in 1905, 3433 in 1935, and, after this picture was taken, BR No 30573. Of the 70 locomotives in this Class, 50 were sold to the Government for use in the Middle East during the First World War and never returned. At nationalisation there were 18 survivors.

Above Drummond Class 'L11' 4-4-0 No 174 photographed on 31 December 1949. It was completed in May 1906 and, most unusually, retains the smokebox wing plates characteristic of L&SWR engines. In the background is an LMS brake-van.

Below One of the first 10 Class 'H15' 4-6-0s of R. W. Urie's design for the L&SWR seen as BR No 30489 on the same day. It was completed at Eastleigh in May 1914. Note the SR-style transfers used for the lettering.

New Cross Gate

New Cross Gate was the oldest motive power depot on the SR, occupying the site of the London & Croydon Railway locomotive works; one building dated from 1844. The shed suffered severe damage during the Second World War and was closed on 14 June 1947, the locomotives being transferred to Bricklayers Arms and Norwood. Despite this, it was still being used for servicing and storing passenger engines when I made my visit on 2 April 1949.

Above A general view of New Cross Gate shed. LB&SCR 1911 'Atlantic', SR No 2425, *Trevose Head*, in lined malachite green livery, has its back to the camera, while the Maunsell 2-6-0 facing it is Class 'N' No 31816 built for the SE&CR in 1922. A number of stored locomotives are visible in the roofless shed in the distance.

Left A Maunsell 'L1' 4-4-0 built by the North British Locomotive Co in 1926. It is shown in malachite green livery and bearing the early BR number S1789 and 'British Railways' in SR-style yellow and black transfers. The chimney is covered to keep rain out. This successful design was an improved version of the SE&CR 1914 'L' Class, the drawings for which were commenced during Wainwright's regime and completed after Maunsell had been appointed. Class 'E' 4-4-0 No 1157, built 1907, stands behind.

Above One of Marsh's famous LB&SCR Class 'I3' 4-4-2Ts, BR No 32084, in elegant hand-painted lettering. This locomotive was built at Brighton in 1912. New Cross Gate station and an 0-6-2T are visible in the background.

Below Stroudley Class 'E1' 0-6-0T, BR No 32142, with a private owner's wagon. This locomotive was built at Brighton in 1879 as No 142 *Toulon*. Between 1874 and 1891 79 members of this goods class were constructed. One of them, No 110 - originally named *Burgundy* - has been preserved on the East Somerset Railway. It survived through having been sold for industrial use in 1927.

Fratton

The LB&SCR opened its line from Havant to Portsmouth on 14 June 1847. Soon afterwards, by an Act of that year, the 4½ miles of line from Hilsea into Portsmouth became the joint property of the LB&SCR and L&SWR. An engine shed was built at Fratton, three-quarters of a mile north-west of what became Portsmouth & Southsea station.

A direct Portsmouth railway from Godalming down to Havant - on the LB&SCR coastal line - was completed in 1858, but it was only on 24 January 1859 after two battles, one a real one with fighting at Havant, and the other a legal one, that the L&SWR started running trains from Waterloo to Portsmouth via the new route. Soon afterwards, the LB&SCR shortened its route to Portsmouth, completing a line from Horsham down to Ford Junction, the 'Mid-Sussex Route', on 3 August 1863, and another from Leatherhead down to Horsham on 1 May 1867.

The Southern Railway electrified the Direct and Mid-Sussex routes to Portsmouth before the Second World War, public services starting on 4 July 1937 and 2 July 1938 respectively. Fratton shed then only supplied passenger locomotives for certain coastal and local (including the Hayling Island branch) services, but continued to supply shunting and goods engines for freight traffic over a wide area.

Stroudley 'Terrier' No 32662 in BR lined black livery at Fratton on 25 March 1950, the day of an ICRS visit. This locomotive, which has been preserved, was built as Class 'A1' No 62 *Martello* at Brighton in 1875 and was rebuilt as Class 'A1X' No 662 in 1913. The coach body used as a cabin would be eagerly sought after nowadays.

Above right Just back from service in the Isle of Wight, 'Terrier' No 32677 in malachite green livery rests inside the shed. This engine was originally No 77 *Wonersh* built at Brighton in 1880. It was rebuilt in 1911 as No 677 of Class 'A1X'. In 1925 it was withdrawn, but two years later was sent to the Isle of Wight as No 3 *Carisbrooke* (renumbered W13 in 1932). It was not one of the 10 'Terriers' to be preserved.

Right One of L. Billinton's handsome LB&SCR Class 'K' 2-6-0s No 32340 in BR lined black livery, the tender carrying the then recently introduced 'lion and wheel' emblem. This particular engine was built in 1914, one of a Class eventually 17 strong. It was withdrawn, with all the others, in 1962.

BRITISH RAILWAYS
32677

32340

Above Drummond L&SWR 'L11' Class 4-4-0 No 441 completed at Nine Elms in May 1907. This engine and No 440 retained their original six-wheeled tenders. The others were later supplied with larger tenders carried by two four-wheel bogies.

Below Fratton was the Southern Region depot equipped with heated storage tanks for fuelling locomotives converted to burn oil. Thirty-one Southern locomotives were so converted under a scheme announced in 1946 and abandoned in September 1947. The two in this picture are 'T9' 4-4-0s Nos 731 and - farther from the camera - 303. These locomotives were built for the L&SWR in 1900 and 1901 respectively. Although necessitating steam pipes in the tender, to keep the oil fluid, oil-burning had the great advantage of doing away with the ash and clinker of a coal fire, not to mention the labour of transferring tons of coal from the tender to the firebox.

Eastbourne

Eastbourne shed, about half a mile outside the terminus, was built by the LB&SCR in 1911. The company had intended to build a carriage and wagon works also, but local opposition prevented this and the works were built at Lancing. Eastbourne shed was damaged during the Second World War and, by the look of it, not repaired.

My father and I visited Eastbourne on Saturday 25 June 1949, travelling by the 5.05 am London Bridge to Brighton steam train, which left our home station, Epsom, at 6.11 am. We then went from Brighton to Lewes, also by steam, and finally from Lewes to Hampden Park - the first station out of Eastbourne.

Inside the largely roofless shed are R. J. Billinton Class 'E5' 0-6-2T No 2406 (originally No 406 *Colworth*) and D. Earle Marsh 'I1' 4-4-2Ts, rebuilt as Class 'I1X' by Maunsell, Nos 2595 and 2005. The two latter were built in Brighton in 1906 and 1907 and rebuilt in 1927 and 1931 respectively.

R. J. Billinton Class 'D3' 0-4-4T built in 1894 as No 385 *Portsmouth*. Billinton had worked with S. W. Johnson on the MR from 1874 to 1890, and was probably influenced by the 0-4-4Ts that Johnson had designed for the GER and MR when designing the 'D3s'. The last of the 36 'D3s', No 32390 (originally No 390 *St Leonards*) was withdrawn in 1956.

Above Another Billinton locomotive, Class 'E5' 0-6-2T No 586 *Maplehurst*, built in 1903, is seen here as rebuilt to Class 'E5X' by Marsh in 1911 with a 'C3' boiler. The British Railways lettering and number are in SR-style transfers. Four of the 30 engines of Class 'E5' were rebuilt in this way.

Below An unobstructed view of an 'I1X' 4-4-2T, No 2009. This was built by Marsh in 1907 and rebuilt by Maunsell in 1929. Amongst other changes a larger boiler (as for a 'B4' or 'I3') was fitted and the cab roof altered to allow passage through the Ore tunnel near Hastings.

Above Standing under a relic of the shed is Class 'B4' 4-4-0 No 2063. This was built at Brighton to the design of R. J. Billinton in 1901 as No 63, and was named *Pretoria* after the town in South Africa where there was fighting during the Boer War.

Below An L. B. Billinton Class 'B4X' 4-4-0 with its early BR number S2060. It was built in 1922 using the bogie and minor parts from the R. J. Billinton Class 'B4' 4-4-0 No 60 *Kimberley* of 1901. The serpentine splasher of the bogie wheels was an unusual feature.

Above Wainwright Class 'D' 4-4-0 No 31490 at Lewes on the train in which my father and I had travelled from Brighton. Note the SR-style transfers used for all the lettering. This locomotive was SE&CR No 490 built at Ashford in 1902. No 737 of the same Class is preserved as part of the National Collection.

Below On our return home we travelled into Eastbourne from Hampden Park in the train shown in the middle of this picture. The locomotive is Class 'I3' 4-4-2T No 32023, built at Brighton in 1908 to D. Earle Marsh's design. This was the superheated locomotive that performed so much better than the saturated-steam LNWR 'Precursor' Class 4-4-0 No 7 *Titan* in working the 'Sunny South Express' between Rugby and Brighton in November 1909. The branch-line train in the far platform is headed by a Class 'E5' 0-6-2T.

5. Signals

The first semaphore signal in Great Britain was installed at New Cross, on the Croydon Railway, by Mr (later Sir) Charles Hutton Gregory in 1841. The arm, pivoted at the top of a slotted post, had three positions: horizontal for 'Danger'; inclined downwards at 45° for 'Caution'; and vertical (when it occupied the slot in the post and became invisible) for 'Clear'. A lamp that rotated when the arm was moved showed red for 'Danger', green for 'Caution' and white for 'Clear'. Interestingly, the NER used slotted posts for its signals right up to the Grouping of 1923, but these were two-position signals of which the arms were horizontal or inclined at 45°, and were never accommodated within the posts.

From the beginning, signal arms were painted red at the front and white at the back. Arms for different purposes were distinguished by stripes, spots, bands, letters and numbers of various colours. In 1872 the LB&SCR adopted a notch for the end of the arm of a Distant signal, and after the First World War it became usual to paint such an arm yellow with a black fishtail stripe across it towards the end.

Many details of signal design varied according to the manufacturer and it was possible to diagnose the owner of a particular stretch of line by looking at the signals. After the First World War, three of the 'Big Four' companies - the exception being the GWR - started to instal upper quadrant signals. They had the advantage that if the arm was forced downwards by a weight of snow or ice, it would indicate 'Danger' rather than 'Clear'. Semaphore signals have now been almost entirely replaced by colour light signals.

The former MR signal gantry at Derby, photographed on 5 May 1950. *AD*

DEVONS ROAD
W680

Left Fowler Class '4F' 0-6-0 goods No 44381 pulls a train of passenger stock across the electrified lines of the District Line to Upminster at Bromley station on 11 June 1949. The full-sized signal arms are of MR pattern, which is not surprising since the MR took over the LT&SR in 1912.

Right Typical LNWR signals, with corrugated metal arms mounted near the top of their posts, at the south end of Rugby station on 26 October 1949. Between the main post of the signal and the Stanier Class '5' locomotive is a glimpse of the girder bridge that carried the former GCR main line from Marylebone to Leicester over the main line from Euston.

Left Characteristic NER signals with wooden arms mounted in slotted wooden posts to the north-west of Appleby East station on the Kirkby Stephen to Penrith line, which closed for passengers on 22 January 1962. *AD*

A wonderful array of NER signals at Barnard Castle, on the Darlington-Kirkby Stephen line and junction for the branch to Middleton-in-Teesdale. Both line and branch closed on 30 November 1964. The old-style level crossing with gates is also impressive. The day when this picture was taken - 6 September 1954 - was not particularly warm, as the smoke coming from the right-hand chimney of the signal box shows. *AD*

Above GNR somersault signals with lattice metal posts on either side of a level crossing at New Bolingbroke on the Lincoln to Skegness line, photographed on 18 September 1962. The arms were pivoted about their midpoints, so that ice or snow along their length had no turning moment that could cause a false 'Clear' indication.

Right Signals nicknamed 'Gog' and 'Magog' at Neasden South box, which controlled the junction between the GCR London Extension (veering away to the right) and the line to Northolt Junction on the GW&GC Joint line through Princes Risborough, diverging to the left. They were photographed on 27 September 1952. *AD*

Left An ex-LB&SCR junction signal at Streatham Common station on the Victoria-Brighton line. The line to the right leads to Streatham station on the London Bridge to Mitcham Junction line, part of the Mid-Sussex route to the South Coast. The white diamonds told the driver of a train waiting at the signal above that his presence was indicated to the signalman on an electrical instrument by means of by track circuits. Photograph taken on 23 November 1949.

Below left One of three fine ex-LB&SCR signals that used to grace the platform ends of the old Epsom Downs station. The arms at the top of the posts served as platform indicators for the drivers of incoming trains. The small arm on the right is a 'Calling on' signal, which allowed a train to pass the top home signal at danger and enter the platform behind a train already present. This picture was taken on 12 February 1950. A housing estate has been built on the site of this station and a small single-platform station nearer to Banstead opened on 14 February 1989.

Below Comparison with the picture on the left shows that the Saxby & Farmer signals on the Metropolitan Railway were closely similar to those on the LB&SCR. The disc shunting signals will have been later additions. This picture was taken on 8 April 1951 at the east end of Rickmansworth station and includes one of the Thompson Class 'L1' 2-6-4Ts used to take locomotive-hauled Metropolitan trains from Baker Street on to Aylesbury.

Bibliography

Details of locomotives

Locomotives of the LMS Past and Present (Locomotive Pub Co, London)

Aldrich, C. Langley: *Great Eastern Locomotives, Past and Present, 1862-1944* (Author, Brightlingsea, 1944)

Allan, Ian: ABCs of LMS, LNER, GWR and Southern Locomotives (various editions 1943-1947); ABCs of British Railways Locomotives (various editions 1948-1964)

Allen, Cecil J.: *The Stanier Pacifics of the LMS* (Ian Allan, London, 1948)

Bellwood, John, and Jenkinson, David: *Gresley and Stanier: A Centenary Tribute* (HMSO, London, 1976)

Burtt, F.: *LB&SCR Locomotives* (1946); *SE&CR Locomotives* (1947); *L&SWR Locomotives* (ca 1949) (Ian Allan, Staines and London)

Butcher, Alan C. (ed): *Railways Restored* (Ian Allan, Shepperton, 1995)

Casserley, H. C., and Johnston, S. W.: *Locomotives at the Grouping: No 1 Southern Railway* (1965); *No 2 London and North Eastern Railway* (1966); *No 3 London, Midland and Scottish* (1966); *No 4 Great Western Railway* (1966) (Ian Allan, London)

Fox, Peter, and Webster, Neil: *Preserved Locomotives of British Railways* 7th ed (Platform 5 Publishing, Sheffield, 1991)

MacLeod, A. B.: *The McIntosh Locomotives of the Caledonian Railway, 1895-1914* (Ian Allan, Staines, 1944)

Nock, O. S.: *Southern Steam* (David & Charles, Newton Abbot, 1966;

The Locomotives of Sir Nigel Gresley (Longmans Green, London, 1945)

Tee, D. F.: *The Midland Compounds* (RCTS, 1962)

Weight, R. A. H.: *Great Northern Locomotives 1847-1947* (Author, Hastings, 1947)

Wethersett, E. R., and Asher, L. L.: *Locomotives of the LNER: A pictorial record* (Heffer, Cambridge, 1947)

Wildish, G. N.: *Engines of War* (Ian Allan, London, 1946)

Histories and reference works

Bucknall, Rixon: *Our Railway History* 2nd ed (Author, London, 1945)

Burtt, F., and Beckerlegge, W.: *Pullman and Perfection* (Ian Allan, London, 1948)

Daniels, Gerald, and Dench, Les: *Passengers No More* 3rd ed (Ian Allan, London, 1980)

Heap, Christine, and Riemsdijk, John van: *The Pre-Grouping Railways* Part 1 (1972); Part 2 (1980); Part 3 (1985) (HMSO, London)

Jackson, Alan A.: *London's Termini* (David & Charles, Newton Abbot, 1969)

Marshall, C. F. Dendy, and Kidner, Rev R. W.: *History of the Southern Railway* 2 vols, 2nd ed (Ian Allan, London, 1963)

Morgan, Bryan: *Railways: Civil Engineering* (Arrow, London, 1973)

Rolt, L. T. C.: *Isambard Kingdom Brunel* (Penguin, Harmondsworth, 1970)

Railway Clearing House: *British Railways Sectional Maps* (Ian Allan, London, ca 1948)

References used for specific sections of the book

Introduction

Essen, R. I.: *Epsom's Hospital Railway* (Author, 1991); Plant, K. P.: *The Ashover Light Railway*, rev ed (Oakwood Press, Oxford, 1987); *Railway Magazine* - Jackson, Alan A.: Oct 1981 pp 478-9

Basingstoke

Waters, Laurence: *Rail Centres: Reading* (Ian Allan, London, 1990)

Bluebell Railway

Railway Magazine - Lee, Charles E.: Jan 1950 pp 44-52; Riley, R. C.: Oct 1954 pp 665-673, Apr 1962 pp 223-230; Spence, Jeoffry: July 1955 pp 461-467; Thomas, Peter: Mar 1986 pp 146-148; Wells, C. F.: May 1950 pp 291-298; Aug 1955 p 549; Oct 1956 p 601; and Mar 1967 p 153. *Railway World* - Johnstone, Steven: Feb 1991 pp 77-81; Sullivan, A. J.: Mar 1981 pp 126-127

Bournemouth

Klapper, Charles F.: *Trains Illustrated* Summer 1967 pp 7-11; *Railway Magazine* - Webb, David R.: Aug 1953 pp 549-556

Bromsgrove

Casserley, H. C.: *The Lickey Incline* 2nd ed rev Jenkins, Stanley C. (Oakwood Press, Oxford, 1990); Ellis, C. Hamilton: *The Midland Railway* (Ian Allan, London, 1966); Gordon, W. J.: *Our Home Railways, Part 2 - The Midland* (Frederick Warne, London); Larkin, Edgar: *An Illustrated History of British Railways' Workshops* (OPC, 1992); *Railway Magazine* - Clinker, C. R.: July 1954 pp 445-454, 472; Sept 1956 pp 575-581; Oct 1956 pp 663-7; Skillern, William J.: July 1953 pp 445-7, 482. *Steam Days* - Harrison, Derek: Aug 1993 pp 436-445

Devons Road

Railway Magazine - Casserley, H. C.: Oct 1951 pp 660-5; May/June 1946 p 195; Apr 1951 p 283

Eastbourne
Railway Magazine - Stones, H. R.: Nov 1953 pp 723-730; Weight, R. A. H.: Jan 1951 p 67

Edinburgh
Mullay, A. J.: *Rail Centres: Edinburgh* (Ian Allan, Shepperton, 1991); Paxton, Roland (ed): *100 Years of the Forth Bridge* (Thomas Telford, London, 1990); Scott-Moncrieff, G.: *Edinburgh* 2nd ed (B. T. Batsford, London, 1948). *BackTrack* - Mullay, A. J. Jan/Feb 1993 pp 19-24. *Railway Magazine* - Sutherland, James H.: Jan 1939 pp 1-5, Mar 1939 pp 196-7; Vallance, H. A.: Mar 1950 pp 147-150; Nov/Dec 1948 pp 414-5; July 1967 pp 366-371; Dec 1990 p 877. *Steam Days* - Morrison, Brian: Dec 1993 pp 631-637

Fratton
British Railways Illustrated - Hardy, R. H. N.: Jan 1995 pp 184-196. *Railway Magazine* - Sekon, G. A.: Jan/Feb 1946 pp 14-20; Mar/Apr 1946 pp 97-9; May/June 1946 pp 147-150; Mar/Apr 1947 pp 105-8; May/Jun 1947 pp 167-8; Aug 1938 pp 102-9; July/Aug 1948 p 212. *Railway World* - Kirkby, J. R. W.: Aug 1988 pp 470-3

Hatfield/Dunstable/Leighton Buzzard
Woodward, Sue, and Woodward, Geoff: *The Hatfield, Luton and Dunstable Railway (and on to Leighton Buzzard)'* 2nd ed (Oakwood Press, Oxford, 1994)

Hayling Island
Railway Magazine - Kennett, Michael J. C.: Sept 1963 pp 599-603; Sekon, G. A.: May/June 1947 pp 167-8, 175. *Steam Days* - Bird, John H.: Dec 1993 pp 639-647

Hellifield
Steam Days - Wilson, Andrew R.: Nov 1992 pp 567-575

Horsham-Guildford
Hodd, H. R.: *The Horsham-Guildford Direct Railway* (Oakwood Press, Blandford, 1975); *Railway Magazine* - Vallance, H. A.: Sept 1950 pp 584-7

Isle of Wight
Robbins, Michael: *The Isle of Wight Railways* (Oakwood Press, Lingfield, 1974); *Railway Magazine* - Gentry, P. W.: Jun 1952 pp 413-8; Jones, K. Westcott: Mar/Apr 1946 pp 112-5; July/Aug 1946 pp 241-5; May/June 1947 pp 144-9; July/Aug 1948 pp 215-8; Riley, R. C.: Feb 1956 pp 75-82; Robbins, Michael: Aug 1954 pp 564-8, 575; Mar 1967 p 154. *Railway World* - Mar 1969 p 134

Kent & East Sussex
Garrett, Stephen: *The Kent and East Sussex Railway* 2nd ed (Oakwood Press, Headington, 1987); *Railway Magazine* - Vallance, H. A.: Feb 1935 pp 105-111; White, H. P.: Aug 1957 pp 525-531. *Railway World* - Shaw, Philip: Jan 1976 pp 34-6. *Steam Days* - Apr 1994 pp 200-211

King's Cross Main Line
Meccano Magazine - Mar 1948 pp 84-6. *Railway Magazine* - May 1952 p 352; Feb 1954 pp 131-2; Aug 1957 pp 579-581

Longmoor Military Railway
Mitchell, Vic, and Smith, Keith: *Branch Lines to Longmoor* (Middleton Press, Midhurst, 1987); Transportation Centre, Royal Engineers: Souvenir Programmes 2 Sept 1950 and 5 Sept 1953; *Meccano Magazine* - Sept 1946 pp 360-1. *Railway Magazine* - Nov/Dec 1946 pp 362-4, 375

Minehead
Mitchell, Vic, and Smith, Keith: *Branch Line to Minehead* (Middleton Press, Midhurst, 1990)

Neasden
Bruce, J. Graeme: *Steam to Silver* (London Transport Executive, 1970)

New Cross Gate
Railway Magazine - Jan/Feb 1948 p.59

Paddington Main Line
Waters, Laurence: *Rail Centres: Reading* (Ian Allan, London, 1990)

Signals
Railway Magazine - Lascelles, T. S.: July/Aug 1945 pp 215-8; Sept/Oct 1945 pp 261-2, 304; Nov/Dec 1945 pp 345-8

Stratford-on-Avon
Dunn, J. M.: *The Stratford-upon-Avon and Midland Junction Railway* (Oakwood Press, 1952); *Railway Magazine* - Beacock, D. A.: Apr 1956 pp 227-230; Robbins, Michael: Aug 1952 pp 512-4. Feb 1935 pp 113-8; Aug 1937 p 131

St Pancras Main Line
Nicholson, Christopher P., and Barnes, Peter: *Railways in the Peak District* (Dalesman, Clapham, 1971)

Tonbridge
Kidner, R. W.: *The Reading to Tonbridge Line* (Oakwood Press, Blandford, 1974); Mitchell, Vic, and Smith, Keith: *Redhill to Ashford* (Middleton Press, 1990)

Uttoxeter-Buxton
Goode, C. T.: *The Ashbourne to Buxton Railway* (Author, Hull, 1990); Rimmer, A.: *The Cromford & High Peak Railway* (Oakwood Press, Headington, 1985)

Wensleydale Branch
Goode, C. T.: *The Wensleydale Branch* (Oakwood Press, 1980); Hallas, C. S.: *The Wensleydale Railway* (Dalesman, Clapham, 1984); Jenkins, Stanley C.: *The Wensleydale Branch - A New History* (Oakwood Press, Headington, 1993); *Railway Magazine* - Abbot, Stan: Apr 1991 pp 258-263; Vallance, H. A.: Oct 1950 pp 661-5; July 1954 p 480

Index

Photographic locations

Locomotive types

Pre-Grouping classes are given their post-Grouping class and/or power designations, where these are different

LMS Group